Melody Wren's

Tea Rooms
of Southern Ontario

Melody Wren's
Tea Rooms
of Southern Ontario

The BOSTON
MILLS PRESS

CANADIAN CATALOGUING IN PUBLICATION DATA

Wren, Melody
Melody Wren's Tea rooms of Southern Ontario

Includes index.
ISBN 1-55046-201-6

1. Restaurants – Ontario, Southern – Guidebooks.
I. Title. II. Title: Tea rooms of Southern Ontario.

TX907.5.C22064 1997   647.95713   C97-930695-7

© 1997 Melody Wren
Cover painting and interior illustrations © 1997 Mary Firth

First published in 1997 by
The Boston Mills Press
132 Main Street
Erin, Ontario
N0B 1T9
Tel 519 833-2407
Fax 519 833-2195

An affiliate of
Stoddart Publishing Company Ltd.
34 Lesmill Road
North York, Ontario, Canada
M3B 2T6

Design by Mary Firth
Printed in Canada

The publisher gratefully acknowledges the support of the Canada Council and
Ontario Arts Council in the development of writing and publishing in Canada.

Boston Mills Press books are available for bulk purchase for sales promotions,
premiums, fundraising, and seminars. For details contact:

Special Sales Department, Stoddart Publishing Co. Limited
34 Lesmill Road, North York Ontario M3B 2T6
Tel 416 445-3333 Fax 416 445-5967

Contents

FOREWORD

A handy guide to wonderful tea experiences in Ontario tea rooms — this is certainly a project that is long overdue! Tea drinkers crave a good cup of tea when they're away from home, but unfortunately, finding that great cuppa too often poses a challenge. The good news is that Melody Wren has done a valuable bit of detective work for tea lovers and has scouted out establishments that treat tea with care, attention and respect.

Properly prepared quality tea is a simple pleasure, one that is growing in popularity as people become more adventurous in their tea selections. At the Tea Council of Canada, we're dedicated to improving the preparation and service of quality tea. So naturally, we're delighted that this guide is now available to help Canadians dis–cover the world of tea — its variety, its taste and aroma and all its soothing qualities — in tea rooms of all kinds, quaint or fancy, Victorian or trendy. The following pages are a superb road map for tea lovers eager to discover the Ontario countryside in pursuit of the world's most popular beverage. Bon voyage!

Danielle J. O'Rourke, President, Tea Council of Canada

The Tea Council of Ontario is a not-for-profit organization of leading tea companies and producing countries, including Sri Lanka, Kenya and India, that is dedicated to the promotion of quality tea to Canadians. For more information on tea, the Tea Council of Canada and its activities, please write to Tea Council of Canada, 885 Don Mills Road, Suite 301, Don Mills, Ontario, M3C 1V9, or fax us at (416) 510-8044.

INTRODUCTION

When I first started my own personal "Year of Tea, Scones and Bread Pudding," I stuck to just the facts, accurately describing each tea room, with a token smattering of detail about the decor, and listing services offered. However, I soon found myself regaling friends and family with tales of tea rooms, sometimes lavishly portraying the tea rooms, the people I met, and the surrounding areas — most of them wonderful, a few not so, that you won't be reading about. So, to avoid sounding like the Saxon Chronicles, which for many years described the unfortunate interaction with the Vikings as "went to battle today, fought the Vikings, lost thirty men; next day, fought Vikings, lost forty more men," I have taken it many steps further, and describe, elaborate and occasionally embellish in my efforts to bring to life these many tea rooms.

On my numerous tea room visits, I usually tried to explore the neighbouring area as well as the tea room itself to get an idea of what else there is to see. I have found lots of wonderful places — antique stores, fabulous, to-die-for secondhand clothing shops, one-of-a-kind bookstores and more. If I've found something unique that excited me, I want to share it with you.

My gastronomic horizons (and my hips) have broadened considerably this year. When I began my tea journey, I was under the illusion that a tea room is a tea room is a tea room. Not so! They are as different from one another as the types of tea they serve, as diverse as their owners, and as unique as each homemade scone. There are friendly, neighbourhood-café tea rooms; pleasant, sun-drenched,

> Surely every one is aware of the divine pleasures which attend a wintry fireside: candles at four o'clock, warm hearthrugs, tea, a fair tea-maker, shutters closed, curtains flowing in ample draperies to the floor, whilst the wind and rain are raging audibly without.
>
> Thomas de Quincey, *Confessions of an Opium-Eater*

take-your-mom tea rooms; all the way to posh, I-wish-I-didn't-have-these-clunky-winter-boots-on tea rooms; and a whole lot in between.

I have been writing about food for half of my life, and given that experience and my passion for cooking (and eating), I seem to have evolved into somewhat of a foodie, food snob — a critic, if you will. However, these tea rooms were not being reviewed, per se, but simply described from my own personal experience, so that you would know exactly what to expect. If you drive two and a half hours to get to a tea room because of what I have written, I don't want you to be disappointed. If there are a few minor glitches, I will mention them. If there are gigantic faux pas, well . . . for one reason or another, some tea rooms never made it to these pages. If I went to tea rooms and they failed me miserably (and I was lenient to a point), I'm afraid they're not in the book. Still, to be fair, I did tell them in advance that I was coming — not to warn them, but so that the owner would save time to chat to me, so they could have used a teapot that wasn't cracked, or one that had a matching lid, or used a tea cosy that hadn't been stained by thousands of tea spills, gossiped about another tea room, or waited to clank the dishes in the adjacent kitchen that had whining, clunking pipes, until after I left — but no, some couldn't, so I didn't.

I visited about 125 tea rooms across Southern Ontario, but about half of the tea rooms I visited were not found in the phone book. Often I would start out the day with an exact list of where I was heading, but after chatting with various people — tea room owners, customers — I would end up adding a few more destinations to the list. If you open a tea room or if we have missed your favourite, don't forget to write. We may want to include it in the next edition.

I have enjoyed each and every morsel of this tea journey, as I hope you will enjoy your tea adventure. Remember to take life sip by sip, not gulp by gulp!

ACKNOWLEDGMENTS

Heartfelt thanks to my family and friends, who out of the goodness of their hearts tirelessly accompanied me on these many tea room visits for the tasks of relaxing and sampling the delicious fare the tea rooms of Southern Ontario have to offer: Gene Brailsford, Christine Bretherick, Mike and Irene Dennison, Jane Gent, Connie and Bill Patterson, Maire Pratschke, Roseanne Sylvestro, Donna Wren, Janet Wright-Smit, Leah Wright, Stephen Lee Wright.

Thanks, too, to my big brothers, Tony and Christopher Digby, for their unwavering interest and support, and my mom, Connie Patterson, for her unconditional support and love.

Appreciation to friends, who each in their own way made a contribution to this tea journey, sometimes more than they know — Stephen Hohenadel, Carol Ann and Chris Sorbara, Sue Norman, Judy Cressman, Sue Silhanek, Fernanda Clark, and Alastair and Catherine Summerlee.

And a special thank you to my most frequent tea-table mate, Jeffrey, who not only drank endless cups of tea, listened to my tea tales, and took photographs, but also drove hundreds of kilometres all over Southern Ontario, and to my wonderfully sweet children, Brendan and Sara, who greeted a most disruptive and unusual year with enthusiasm and support. (Sara sometimes took scones and Devon cream to school for lunch!)

Warm thanks to John Denison, my publisher, who nursed the project along with enthusiasm from the beginning, and to my patient editor, Kathleen Fraser. Thanks also to Mary Firth, for her wonderful design and illustrations.

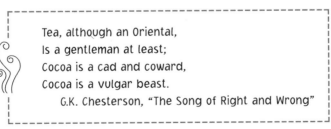

Tea, although an Oriental,
Is a gentleman at least;
Cocoa is a cad and coward,
Cocoa is a vulgar beast.
   G.K. Chesterson, "The Song of Right and Wrong"

WHY TEA?

Thivs book came about because so many exciting things are happening with tea. Tea rooms are popping up all over Canada. In each province, tea rooms are experiencing a resurgence, many in villages one might never have discovered but continue to be delighted with, once found.

Canadians drink more than seven billion cups of tea per year. According to the Tea Council of Canada, approximately 88 percent of adult Canadians drink tea, either hot or iced; 48 percent of tea drinkers are men, 52 percent are women. In the January 1995 issue of *Quarterly Clips*, produced by the Tea Council of Canada, an article called "Tea Consumption, Boiling in Canada" notes: "Maybe it's the growing population of seniors, or perhaps higher prices for coffee. Or just the need to find a few minutes of comfort in a stressed–out world. Whatever the reason, tea consumption is on the rise."

An important factor contributing to the popularity of tea is the increasing health consciousness of consumers. Tea is an all–natural beverage. Recent research shows that tea consumption has been associated with improved cardiovascular health and may help protect against certain forms of cancer. Research from Rutgers University in New Jersey indicates that three cups of tea a day may help prevent cancer, particularly of the skin.

Hot or cold, fresh brewed tea without milk or sugar contains no calories, no additives or preservatives, and is naturally low in caffeine.

Tea in its 1990s' incarnation is for people who are interested in "having tea" as a form of entertainment. Afternoon tea is a moment of tranquillity and sweet stillness, a time to truly savour a reviving cup of tea. In the continuing quest for the ideal beverage, cen-

turies–old tea scores new points for good taste, economy (three cents per cup), intriguing complexity and variety. Having tea is a delightful, wondrous escape amid a takeout, Styrofoam–serving, drive–through world. Some people are cutting back working hours and seeking voluntary simplicity in a search for their souls and their happiness. For others, gentler times can be found in the quiet ambience of a tea room, sharing a pot of tea and a cosy chat with a friend.

A BRIEF HISTORY OF TEA

The story of tea is a wondrous one, weaving its way through many countries, centuries and lives, from the early days in China to its place today as Britain's national beverage and one that is fast rising in popularity in North America. Tea has played a part in British history since the mid–1600s, and its story in the Far East goes back much further than that.

Various legends tell of the discovery of tea. The Indian and Japanese stories both attribute it to Bodhidharma, the devout Buddhist priest who founded Zen Buddhism. The Indian legend tells how the priest was in the fifth year of a seven–year, sleepless contemplation of Buddha when he began to feel drowsy. He plucked a few leaves from a nearby bush and chewed them, immediately dispelling his sleepiness. The bush was, of course, a wild tea tree. The Japanese version has it that he was so angry with his eyes for closing in sleep that he sliced off his eyelids and cast them to the ground. Where they fell a bush grew, producing leaves that had the effect of increasing alertness and restoring energy.

In the Chinese legend, the Emperor Shen Nung, a scholar and herbalist, was boiling his drinking water one day when he noticed that a few leaves had fallen into the pot from an overhanging tree. He was aware of a pleasant and appetizing smell wafting from the pot, and when he drank the liquid, found it to have restorative powers. In the story, Shen Nung's herbal experiment dates back to 2750 B.C., but

the first references to tea do not appear until about the fourth century A.D. Toward the middle of the Tang dynasty, in about A.D. 780, tea became the subject of a specialized book, *Ch'a Ching*, which gave instruction on every aspect of the growing, preparing and drinking of tea. On the matter of suitable daily consumption, readers were informed that "For exquisite freshness and vibrant fragrance, limit the number of cups to three. If one may be satisfied with less than perfection, five are permissible."

In each of these countries, tea has become a popular beverage, initially drunk for its medicinal properties and not as a refreshing indulgence. Indeed, the early brew would have had a rather bitter taste, since only the green leaves were used at first. (The process of fermentation and producing black tea as we know it was not developed until about A.D. 650.

From China, tea was carried to Japan by a Buddhist scholar in the ninth century A.D., but until the late sixteenth century, no European, apart from a few explorers, had heard of tea. The Portuguese and the Dutch were the first tea traders, transporting regular shipments of the new herb to the ports of France and the Baltic coast in 1610. Small amounts probably came to Britain through travelling merchants and members of the court taking journeys, but there is no record of tea being sold in England before 1658. The name "tea" derives from the Chinese word *T'e*, or *Tcha* in Cantonese. In its early years in Britain, it was referred to as "tay" or "tee" (pronounced "tay" until about 1711), and cheap black tea was known as "bohea."

With the cargoes of tea arrived teapots and bowls from China and Japan. The quality of the fine porcelain thrilled European potters, who spent the next hundred years trying to perfect the manufacture of a similar material. It was in the 1660s that the word "china" was first used to encompass all the plates, bowls, saucers, jars and dishes imported from the Orient.

In 1660, Thomas Garaway, the shrewd owner of the Sultaness Head, a famous London coffee house, placed an advertisement in the *London Gazette* for the latest and most fashionable drink — tea. He hailed its arrival in the city by claiming that consumers of this wondrous new beverage would find a miraculous cure for "headache, stone, gravel, dropsy, scurvy, sleepiness, loss of memory, looseness or gripping of the guts, heavy dreams, and collick proceeding from wind." Furthermore, he assured his customers, "if you are of corpulent body it ensures good appetite, and if you have a surfeit it is just the thing to give you a gentle vomit." With such recommendations, it is no wonder that the fashion for tea swept Europe in the seventeenth century.

THE TEA BAG ACCIDENT

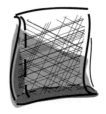

Tea bags developed quite by accident in 1904 when a tea merchant, anxious to acquire new customers, sent out samples of his teas wrapped in small silk bags. Not knowing how else to handle them — and assuming they were doing the correct thing — a few of his customers put the bags in cups or pots, poured on the boiling water, and presto, a new marketing idea was born. Selling tea wrapped in silk was not a money-making venture, and silk soon gave way to a gauze material. Most of today's bags are neither of silk nor of gauze but of a specially treated filter paper.

A TEA GLOSSARY

Chinese mystic of the T'ang Dynasty wrote, "The first cup of tea moistens my lips and throat. The second shatters my loneliness. The third causes the wrongs of life to fade gently from my recollection. The fourth purifies my soul. The fifth lifts me to the realms of the unwinking gods."

There are three main types of tea: green, black and oolong. All three types come from the tea plant, *Camellia sinensis*, but they are processed differently. Green tea is produced when the leaves are fired (steamed and dried) immediately after picking. Firing inactivates enzymes present in the tea leaf and stops the natural oxidation process that takes place after picking. In the production of black tea, the leaves are allowed to oxidize before firing, resulting in a darkening of leaf colour and a change in aroma. Oolong teas are semi-oxidized, which gives them a flavour that is stronger than green teas, but more delicate than black teas. White teas are very rare teas produced exclusively in China; they are made from only the tip of the tea plant.

In Canada, black tea is favoured, while green tea is preferred in Asia and parts of the Middle East. Green tea is growing in popularity because of its health benefits.

BLACK TEAS

Assam
Grown in the northeast Assam region of India. Bright colour with full-bodied malt taste.

English Breakfast
Traditionally a blend of China Keemuns. Today the blend has evolved to include Ceylon and India teas to produce a full-bodied brew.

Darjeeling
Known as the "champagne of tea."
Grown in the foothills of the Himalayas, with a subtle flowery bouquet and a delicate muscatel flavour.

Ceylon Breakfast
A blend of fine teas grown on the hillsides of Sri Lanka, producing a rich golden liquor with superb flavour.

Keemun
A fine black tea from China, sometimes used in English Breakfast. It has a dark amber colour.

Orange Pekoe

A term denoting a large-leaf tea, often confused for an orange-flavoured blend.

Lapsang Souchong

A large-leaf China Black tea with a distinctive smoky flavor resulting from its unique drying process.

Irish Breakfast

A blend of black teas from Assam, Ceylon and East Africa. A robust and full-bodied tea.

Russian Caravan

A blend of China Black teas.

Earl Grey

An aromatic afternoon tea, a blend of fine black teas flavoured with oil of bergamot.

OOLONG TEAS

Black Dragon

A delicate fruity tea from the Amoy, Foochow and Canton Provinces of China and Taiwan.

China Oolong

A select blend of large-leaf teas from both China and Taiwan with an exquisite flavour and fragrant aroma of fresh peaches.

Mainland Oolong

Often scented with jasmine and gardenia, it has a nutty taste.

Formosa Oolong

Known for its peach flavour and aroma, according to Schapira's delightful 1975 *Book of Coffee and Tea*, this is "the champagne of teas," "liquid sunshine," and "the philosopher's drink."

GREEN TEAS

Gunpowder

Grown in China and Taiwan, this tea has a clear yellow-green color and a slightly bittersweet taste. Easily recognized by its round pellet shape, and made from young leaves rolled into balls, hence its name.

Hyson

A pan-fired green tea, with a fragrant, bitter taste.

Imperial

A green tea made from rolled leaves.

Jasmine

A delicate blend of China green teas scented with white jasmine petals, producing a light, subtle liquor with a mild sweet flavour.

WHITE TEAS

These rare teas have a pale golden colour when brewed, and are prized for their mellow, slightly sweet flavour.

TEA TIPS FOR COMMONERS

Does one add milk before or after pouring the tea in the cup?

This is entirely a matter of preference. However, it seems that the milk mixes better with the tea if the milk is poured in first. It is thought that the "milk first" rule came about to prevent delicate porcelain from being cracked by the scalding hot tea. However, Queen Elizabeth II is said to prefer adding the milk after her tea is poured.

Should one raise a pinkie when drinking tea?

Among the many Victorian rules at teatime — such as not gossiping, not discussing surgery, looking away if one dropped a sugar cube — it was considered very vulgar to discuss money. But a shrewd observer could always tell: if one came from old money, the pinkie was crooked; if one came from new money, the pinkie was extended straight up; if one had no money, one had to crook and pretend!

The addition of a handle on the teacup was an English design and was born of necessity — it made it easier to hold the cup. This happened sometime in the late seventeenth or early eighteenth century. Holding out the pinky finger was de rigueur because the cups were so small that there simply wasn't room for all of the fingers. Cups are bigger now, and so the custom varies between generations. One person thinks it is elegant; the next thinks it a scandalous affectation.

What is clotted cream, or Devon cream?

Throughout this guide book, you may notice my passion for Devon cream, and my feeling that a scone is not complete without it. Real clotted or Devon cream, sometimes called double Devon cream, is a thick, rich yellow cream famous to the West Country of England. It is lavishly dolloped on scones, cakes, fresh fruit salad, pies — practically

> "And I don't know if I am doing right — it may make you more addlepated than ever — but you can ask Diana to come over and spend the afternoon with you and have tea here."
>
> "Oh Marilla!" Anne clasped her hands. "How perfectly lovely! You are able to imagine things after all or else you'd never have understood how I've longed for that very thing."
>
> I can just imagine myself sitting down at the head of the table and pouring out the tea," said Anne, shutting her eyes ecstatically. "And asking Diana if she takes sugar! I know she doesn't but of course I'll ask her just as if I didn't know."
>
> L.M. Montgomery, *Anne of Green Gables*

every sweet or pudding enjoyed. Once you've been served Devon cream in a tea room, you'll look for it again and again. Made in huge quantities commercially, this delicious cream is shipped all over.

Equally scrumptious is farmhouse clotted cream, a handmade cream that tends to be a richer yellow and slightly thicker in consistency than the commercial variety. In many farmhouse kitchens, the clotted cream pan sits on the coal–burning stove waiting patiently for its milky contents to separate. The cream rises to the top of the milk and is skimmed off the top. If you go rambling about the country lanes in some parts of England, you will spot numerous farm gates with handmade signs, Clotted Cream for Sale.

Unless you can get milk straight from the cow, don't bother trying to make clotted cream from Canadian milks and creams — it's hopeless. Devonshire cream is now available in many grocery stores, in the dairy case. If you can't find it, what you can do, so as not to be deprived, is make mock Devon cream (recipe follows). Some diehards insist there is no comparison, but this mock Devon cream is an extremely good substitute, and it makes enough for quite a few scones. It is not the same as clotted cream but is very delicious all the same. This is lovely with ripe berries and is a classic on scones with preserves.

Mock Devonshire Cream

1 c. heavy cream
1 c. sour cream
4 tbsp. confectioners' sugar

Beat cream until stiff peaks form, adding sugar in the last few minutes of mixing. Fold in the sour cream and blend well. Refrigerate. Serve with you know what.

For the Victorians, the best thing to serve with tea was gossip and scandal!

Microwave Lemon Curd

8 tbsp. butter
grated peel of three large lemons
1/2 c. fresh lemon juice
3 large eggs
1 c. granulated sugar

For those of us who love the taste, but don't have time.

In a microwave-safe bowl, microwave butter for about 3 minutes on high until melted. In a separate bowl, whisk together the eggs, sugar, lemon peel and juice until well combined. Whisk into the melted butter. Microwave on high for 2 minutes, whisking often until thick enough to coat a wooden spoon. Store in glass jars in refrigerator for up to 4 weeks — if it lasts that long. Serve with scones and Devon cream, either in place of preserves or alongside to give guests a choice.

no! ne'er was mingled such a draught
In palace, hall or arbor,
As freemen brewed and tyrants quaffed
That night in Boston Harbour.
Oliver Wendell Holmes, "Ballad of the Boston Tea Party"

THE ORIGINS OF ICED TEA

A favourite summer drink for all open-air occasions is iced tea. Iced tea was first introduced by an Englishman, Richard Blechynden, at the St. Louis World's Fair in 1904. Because of the scorching weather, he was unable to sell his hot tea, so he poured it over ice and immediately sold gallons.

In the United States the consumption of iced tea is very high — 80 percent of the tea Americans drink is iced, and 20 percent is hot. In Canada the opposite is true. William Gladstone, the British prime minister, said in 1865, "If you are cold, tea will warm you; if you are heated, it will cool you; if you are depressed, it will cheer you; if you are excited, it will calm you."

I enjoy drinking hot tea in the summer, when the weather is steamy, but here is a recipe for a refreshing iced tea to make if you are heated and prefer it with ice.

Iced Ginger Tea

Make jugs of this to cool guests off. Pack it in a Thermos and take it with your picnic. Instead of using tea bags, use loose tea. (It's actually far less expensive to use loose tea than tea bags.)

1 1/2 tbsp. Darjeeling tea
2 tbsp. grated fresh ginger root
1 tbsp. sugar
2 c. boiling water
1 tbsp. lemon juice
2 c. ice

Place tea, ginger and sugar in heatproof jug or teapot. Pour boiling water over top; allow to rest 5 minutes. Strain tea into pitcher with ice cubes. Stir until ice partially melts. Taste and adjust sugar and lemon juice. Makes 4 drinks.

4 & 20 Blackbirds
Bake Shop and Tea Room

Gayle Allen, owner
Bothwell
519–695–3634

Tuesday through Thursday 10 to 5, Friday 12 to 5, Saturday 10 to 5.

This is a very basic but quaintly decorated bakeshop and tea room in the heart of rural Ontario. The garden is lush with lilac trees, and every tree has a bird feeder on it, so there is a constant stream of birds to watch, making it a delightful spot in which to sample some of Gayle Allen's home baking. There are only three tables in the teal and white bakeshop, but the front porch holds considerably more.

The soup on the menu changes daily — the day we visited it was creamy asparagus — and you can have sandwiches made up for you. The tarts are particularly delicious and include old-fashioned favourites such as butter tarts, and raspberry and coconut, pecan, and black walnut tarts.

What a lovely place to stop on a country drive.

Meanwhile, let us have a cup of tea. The afternoon glow is brightening the bamboos, the fountains are bubbling with delight, the soughing of the pines is heard in our kettle. Let us dream of evanescence, and linger in the beautiful foolishness of things.

Kazuko Okakura, *The Book of Tea*

Turn of the Century Tea Room

Lisa Van Wyck and Ruth Snow, owners
3022 Brigden Road, Brigden
519–864–4460

Monday through Friday 9 to 3, Saturday 8 to 3, closed Sunday.

I t's off the beaten track, but this delightful tea room is well worth the detour. Lisa and Ruth have created a friendly, Victorian–style tea room where you'll feel as welcome as the regulars. When Lisa and Ruth uncovered the dropped ceiling of what was originally a butcher shop, they discovered a beautiful punched–tin ceiling, which they have painted cream and trimmed with burgundy and teal — a beautiful Victorian combination echoed in the wallpaper. The tables are laid with pretty Royal Albert China on cream-coloured cloths. The woodstove in the corner makes this comfortable tea room even cosier in the fall and winter.

See the blackboard for the daily specials: carrot, zucchini or blueberry muffins, daily soups, reunion casserole (noodles, Italian sausage and tomato sauce) with salad and sunflower bread, and a variety of sandwiches.

The Victorian Rose Tea Room

Louise Morrison and Rose Robertson, owners
64 Main Street East, Kingsville
519-733-9035

Daily 11 to 9, open weekend evenings May through October only,
closed winter evenings Monday through Thursday.

You'll find the Victorian Rose in a century clapboard house on the main street of Kingsville. Four rooms, all done in blues and yellows, but each in a different way, are furnished with round tables and black wrought-iron chairs and long tables with church pews. The entire effect is spacious, bright and relaxing.

Menu offerings include tangerine salad with mandarins, fresh greens, and pineapple with a creamy fruit dressing, a ploughman's lunch, Rose's pasta marinara, and crêpes of the day.

An afternoon Devon cream tea is available and includes fresh scones, strawberry preserves with clotted cream, and tea. The English afternoon tea includes delicate cucumber sandwiches with tea. Lunch for two is about $20.

TEAS SERVED: Darjeeling, Jasmine with flowers, and Orange Pekoe. Fruit infusions are also available. All teas are loose except for the Orange Pekoe.

LOCAL INTEREST: Visitors come for the Jack Miner Bird Sanctuary, the Pelee Island Winery, and the Kingsville Railway Station, which was built in 1888 for whisky magnate Hiram Walker.

Bear Creek Food Emporium and Tea Room

Ken Melton, owner
4211 Petrolia Line, Petrolia
519–882–3986

Tuesday to Saturday 11 to 2:30.

One thing I loved about Petrolia is that some innovative person started, three years ago, delivering milk by horse–drawn truck to area homes. The milk is in bottles, too! The old–world ambience of Bear Creek is exactly right for its setting in Petrolia — a charming little town with interesting antique shops and quaint old streets. Ken Melton has created a popular, friendly establishment, where locals regularly drop by for a refreshing cuppa after a shopping trip and where visitors stop off on their way sightseeing.

The comfortable tea room is quite large, but cosy, with a country atmosphere. Walls are filled with framed prints (all for sale) as well as interesting collectibles. The chairs are an eclectic assortment of antiques and reproductions; white lace tablecloths on the tables unify the whole look.

Bear Creek offers a simple menu of sandwiches and daily specials. All the food is homemade and desserts change daily.

"It has never occurred to Mr. Winterbourne to offer me any tea," she said, with her little tormenting manner. "I have offered you advice," Winterbourne rejoined. "I prefer weak tea!"

Henry James, *Daisy Miller*

The Tea Kozee

Debbie Rice, owner
The Old Post Office, 4189 Petrolia Line, Petrolia
519-882-1311

Daily 9 to 2:30.

This unusual tea room is housed in the Old Post Office, an impos-
ing Romanesque Revival building described in the local newspa-
per in 1891 as a "Post Office worthy the town and its acknowledged
wealth." Inside, the style is more eclectic, with post office memorabilia,
a '50s diner counter at the back, and a comfortable front room nicely
decorated in teal and burgundy, with a mix of antique chairs and lots
of original wood.

This is a good tea room for a casual visit with a friend over a
snack and a cup of tea. The menu lists breakfast specials, lunchtime
salads, soups and sandwiches. Other treats offered are brownies,
scones, zabaglione, and miniature mousses served in an eggcup.

 LOCAL INTEREST: Petrolia is the site of the first oil discovery
in Canada. Oil is still pumped in the fields of Petrolia and
nearby oil springs just as it was a hundred years ago. Victoria Hall was
built in 1889, gutted by fire in its its centennial year, and is now completely restored to its former glory. The summer theatre on the top
floor draws many visitors to Petrolia.

> My experience convinced me that tea was better than brandy,
> and during the last six months in Africa, I took no brandy, even
> when sick, taking tea instead.
>
> Theodore Roosevelt (1858–1919), Letter, 1912

Someplace Tea Room

Carol McDonald and Cheryl Parsons, owners
4152 Petrolia Street, Petrolia
519–882–1311

Monday through Saturday 9 to 3:30.

The Someplace Tea Room is Petrolia's "original tea room" and has been in business for the past nine years. This country café–style tea room is decorated in lovely greens, with floral wallpaper, lattice-work on the ceiling and lots of hanging plants.

All the soups and breads are homemade. Daily hot specials such as cabbage rolls, lasagna, chicken stir-fry, and asparagus melts make good lunches, but this tea room is best known for their irresistible baking. You can choose from many differ-ent pies, including coconut cream, glazed strawberry and Dutch apple, or indulge in iced carrot cake, chocolate turtle cheesecake or rhubarb custard.

If it is hot and humid, you may want to order a citrus smoothie; refreshing and delicious, it is a frosty mix of orange juice, grapefruit juice, banana and gingerale.

LOCAL INTEREST: There is so much to see in Petrolia that we stayed overnight at Tully's B & B, one of Ontario's best. It is a beautiful house within walking distance of downtown. Gord and Elizabeth Tully made us very welcome and told many interesting tales about Petrolia, particularly how wealthy the town was in its oil hey-day. Apparently the latest fashions were once shown in Paris, London, Rome and Petrolia!

The Garden Tea House

Olive Archibald, owner
1840 London Road, Sarnia
519–541–0104

Monday through Saturday 10 to 3. Closed the end of August and
beginning of September, after Christmas to the first week of January,
and also the Victoria Day weekend.

The Garden Tea House spreads out through several small, sun–filled rooms on two floors of this charming house built in 1906. Olive Archibald has created a very friendly, country–style tea room, where the tables are laid with pretty white china and fresh flowers, the home–baked cakes and scones are a treat, and every customer is looked after with great care and attention.

Olive is both the owner and the chef, and she has a uniquely healthy approach to the menu. She changes it frequently, offering extensive, imaginative choices using fresh ingredients, and is very careful with the fat content. The food is a real gourmet delight and is beautifully presented. A Polynesian summer salad with a dressing made of a coconut essence has become very popular. You may want to try the brie, fried delicately and served with fruit, homemade brown bread and cranberry sauce.

I had a crab–asparagus quiche with the house salad, tossed with Olive's incredibly delicious raspberry poppyseed dressing, one of several that are available by the bottle. The special that day was B.C. salmon in phyllo pastry with chutney. The bread pudding baked that morning — the best bread pudding I've ever tasted — was dense with lots of raisins and smothered in cream drizzled with warm caramel sauce — totally decadent.

Catering is available, and weddings or dinners for twelve or more can be arranged.

Rose of Sharon Tea Room

Walt and Yvonne Noordam, owners
532 Niagara Street, Wyoming
519-845-0304

Monday through Saturday 11 to 4, closed Mondays in January.

The Rose of Sharon is probably one of the most important tourist attractions in Wyoming, and everyone who has tea here says how wonderful it is. It is housed in an old clapboard house with a large front porch and a garden abundant with flowers.

This elegant yet comfortable tea room is decorated in burgundies and forest greens. Fabulous centrepieces adorning the lace tablecloths are all for sale, as are the local artwork and dried-flower arrangements that deck the walls.

Salads, quiches and sensational sandwiches as well as homemade cheese biscuits and scones make up the menu. Homemade desserts change daily. Walt Noordam is a friendly host, and makes a point of mentioning that the food on the menu has "Walt-sized portions," appealing especially to the male customers.

> What part of confidante has that poor teapot played ever since the kindly plant was introduced among us. Why myriads of women have cried over it, to be sure! What sickbeds it has smoked by! What fevered lips have received refreshment from it! Nature meant very kindly by women when she made the tea plant; and with a little thought, what a series of pictures and groups the fancy may conjure up and assemble round the teapot and cup.
>
> William Makepeace Thackeray, *Pendennis*

Avon Garden Tea Room

A community venture
Avon United Church, Putnam Road, Avon
519-269-3022 or 269-3907 or 269-3970

Thursday through Saturday 11:30 to 2. Reservations for large groups
only; bus tours welcome by reservation for lunch or afternoon tea.

This unique tea room is in the basement of an active church. The utilitarian space is brightened by tablecloths and fresh plants on each table, and by the handmade quilts that hang on the walls. (The quilts are for sale, so if you see one you particularly like . . .) Excellent homemade food and fresh, all-natural teas are served at bargain prices.

The tea room is very much a community effort, and is run by some energetic characters — Brenda Daniel, Sue Lackie, Gwen Tracey and Kathy Collett. Everyone in the room seems to know each other, so there is much laughter and conversation. A percentage of the profits go to the Avon United Church, which is in itself unusual, as the church space is shared by two different denominations. The hours of the tea room are somewhat limited because the women involved all have their own businesses.

The menu board features specials each day. Everything is cooked using fresh herbs from a local herb and herbal products business. Brenda Daniel happens to be a turkey breeder, raising some 16,000 turkeys, hence, she explains with a laugh, the daily turkey special. The

specials that day were turkey terrine with tomato basil glaze served with scalloped potatoes and orange-glazed carrots, and a sweet-and-sour pineapple pork on rice. Specials are served with a garden salad, herb tea-biscuits and a beverage, and portions are hearty. Desserts were a bargain and hard to choose from — rhubarb cheesecake, Black Forest trifle, and home-baked pies, including raisin, pumpkin and tayberry. (A tayberry is a cross between red and black raspberries.) The food was delicious — all freshly baked and artistically served with fresh nasturtiums and fruit.

A small gift shop sells patchwork placemats, napkins and country collectibles, but because the church is used as a church on Sundays, the gift shop reverts to a nursery for the church children. What a wonderful way to employ a seldom-used space!

The Green Frog Tea Room

Brenda Smith, owner
Pinecroft, Rogers Road South, Aylmer
519-773-3435

Open 11 to 3:30 for lunch, tea until 4 every day but Sunday. Closed first two weeks of January.

Brenda Smith's grandfather was a successful butcher eighty-five years ago. Since he had no refrigeration, work slowed in the summer, but he didn't want to lay off his staff, so he had them plant pine trees to fulfill his dream of recreating a piece of Muskoka in Aylmer. They planted 85,000 trees, covering 52 acres and taking seven years in the process. Then he built the cabin, now the tea room, dredged a pond, and built a larger cabin, now a small bed and breakfast, for his wife to read in.

Later the Pinecroft Pottery was started, and eighteen years ago the tea room opened to celebrate the first thirty years of business at the pottery. There were so many pottery classes and Women's Institute groups taking classes, and then craving a cuppa afterward, that Brenda saw a need for the tea room, so opened it on a small scale and kept adding to it.

The cabin housing the tea room and gift shop is now huge, nestled among the towering pines and overlooking the picturesque pond. Hammocks and ingeniously designed lawn chairs scattered about the property may tempt you to sit and relax. Other little cottages house the studios of local artists and gift shops.

The tea room dishware is from the Pinecroft Pottery — each piece is unique and rustic. Even though the room seats eighty-five, it still has a relaxing country-cottage atmosphere. The food is all homemade. Specials on our visit were asparagus pie with cheddar on top, chicken casserole with biscuits, Reuben crêpes, and garden vegetable pie, all served with huge, flaky buns. Dessert specials made for difficult choosing, between bumbleberry pie, apple dumpling served with brown sugar sauce, cherry cheesecake, and ice cream with walnuts.

You may want to ask about the special gourmet dinners, planned for the third Saturday of each month.

 TEAS SERVED: Darjeeling, Earl Grey, English Breakfast, and Jasmine. A variety of herbal and fruit infusions are also available.

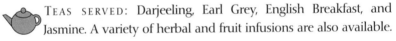

In nothing more is the English genius for domesticity more notably declared than in the institution of this festival — almost one may call it — of afternoon tea . . . The mere chink of cups and saucers tunes the mind to happy repose.

George Gissing, *The Private Papers of Henry Ryecroft*

Mill Pond Corner Tea Room

Dian Naish, owner
32 Stanley Street, Ayr
519-632-8548

Monday through Friday 9 to 4, Saturday and Sunday 10 to 5.

This is more than just a tea room; it is a café that offers an all-day breakfast, catering and takeout, and will do private dinners. The inviting entranceway draws you upstairs to the tea room, where linen walls, glass tables, cane furniture and Tiffany-style lamps lend a wonderful, light ambience.

The lunch menu offers some delicious and out-of-the-ordinary choices, including baked brie spread served with fruit, crackers and a raspberry coulis; smoked salmon with basil cream cheese on pumpernickel; and oat-bread bruschetta with fresh herbs, garlic, tomatoes and onions in olive oil. For lighter fare, try chicken scone pot pie, crêpes or the quiche of the day, all served with homemade bread and salad.

Dietary concerns are given special consideration here. If you tell the server that you would like substitutes for sugar, dairy or wheat, the chef will be glad to incorporate them into your meal. Let your server know if you are in a hurry, as this wholesome food is prepared to order.

You'll be tempted by the fabulous selection of pastries and cakes, warm from the oven — double fudge brownies, home-baked pies, butter tarts, apple dumplings, maple oatmeal cookies, and cheesecake among them.

Afternoon tea is served from 2 P.M. on. A cream tea includes a choice of scone served warm with preserves and cream, and high tea promises dainty sandwiches, sweets and a scone with preserves and cream.

The wholesome quality of the food and the pleasant atmosphere make this an excellent place for lunch or afternoon tea.

Montgomery's Tea Room

Carol Sloan, owner
138 Charing Cross Street, Brantford
519-752-2552

Tuesday through Friday 11:30 to 4, Saturday 11:30 to 3.
Wheelchair accessible.

When you have finished exploring Brantford, it is worth making the journey to find this exquisitely pretty cottage with whitewashed walls and vibrant yellow shutters. The tiny print wallpaper and low ceilings, all in pale greens and pinks, are as homey and cosy as the outside is picturesque. Carol Sloan offers a warm welcome to all visitors.

The menu changes weekly; specials that day were homemade mushroom soup, creamed chicken with veggies on a tea biscuit served with salad and a selection of delicious homemade dressings. For the little guests, there is peanut butter and jam on a croissant, served with veggies and dip.

Devon tea is served after 2 P.M., with tea, scones, jam and fresh cream, for less than $4 per person.

Desserts here will send you into ecstasies. We asked to share a dessert, but fortunately were coaxed to eat a piece of coconut cream pie and Carol's special cheesecake with pineapple and cream, and both were superb. No wonder the tea room was bustling with customers, and many of them regulars.

 LOCAL INTEREST: Visit the Alexander Graham Bell homestead in Brantford.

Cornerstone Inn and Tea Room

Mary Lambert, owner
38 John Street East, Exeter
519-235-3669; toll free 1-888-295-6222

By appointment only, 2 to 3 and 3:15 to 4:15.

This heritage Victorian home, originally built in 1878 and now surrounded by idyllic gardens and an inviting wraparound porch, has been lovingly maintained. Just inside to the left, you'll find Mary Lambert's gift shop, temptingly filled with Battenberg lace, and many items by local artisans. To the right is the tea room, where a burgundy-and-cream colour scheme is carried throughout, from the tablecloths and water glasses to the scatter mats on the original wood floors. The elegant, cosy room is also home to Mary's collection of silver tea services.

A true Victorian tea is served — scones and Devon cream, petits fours, cucumber and watercress sandwiches, salmon and walnut sandwiches and, of course, tea. Low tea — scones, Devon cream and preserves — is also offered.

You'll find this the perfect place to relax after a wander around the area or a ramble in the nearby countryside. Stay for tea, or for a night in one of the well-appointed inn rooms.

For tea, though ridiculed by those who are naturally coarse in their nervous sensibilities, or are become so from wine-drinking, and are not susceptible of influence from so refined a stimulant, will always be the favoured beverage of the intellectual
Thomas de Quincey, *Confessions of an Opium-Eater*

Marsh's General Store and Tea Room

Nancy Pollard, owner
Ilderton
519–666–1034

Wednesday through Friday 11 to 4, Saturday and Sunday 11 to 5.
Wheelchair accessible.

This white clapboard building, built by the Marsh family in 1869, is set beside a conservation area in the middle of the small village of Coldstream, just west of London. A wraparound balcony, bird feeders, and school benches on the front porch present a welcome entranceway, beckoning you inside.

To get to the three small tea rooms, walk through the delightful old-fashioned general store, well stocked with antique china, cards, books and tea accessories. Or go upstairs to find historic paraphernalia from the early days of the store, and rooms displaying antique furniture and china for sale at very reasonable prices.

Choosing a table in one of the tea rooms is no easy task, as they are all equally pleasant. Pretty floral cloths on round tables, original pine floors, antique bentwood chairs, and classical music make this a cosy place. Outside each window is a different bird feeder, and we were entertained by a parade of colourful birds as we sipped our tea — cardinals, finches, bluejays and many we did not know. In warm weather you can enjoy your tea outside, on the upper balcony or on the front lawn.

The tea room menu varies, with daily specials such as shepherd's pie, beef barley soup, and salad with mango, melon and avocado dressing. Afternoon tea is country-style, with home-baked biscuits (plain or cheese), apple butter or preserves, and a choice of tea. Mouth-watering choices on the "Definitely Dessert" menu include nectarine blueberry pie, strawberry-lime mousse tart with cookie crust, mocha-

chocolate confetti cake, and apple galette.

If you call a day ahead, Marsh's will custom-package a picnic lunch for you — perfect for taking to the lovely conservation area next door. They also have rooms available for special occasions and meetings.

Lunch was delightful and very reasonable; lunch for two with tea, soup, salads, biscuits and desserts was about $20.

The Clog and Thistle Tea Room

Catherine Van Dyke, owner
189 Thames Street South, Ingersoll
519-425-0900

Tuesday through Sunday 11 to 9. Reservations are encouraged.
Wheelchair accessible.

This is one of the largest tea rooms I have come across. It seats a hundred people in five separate rooms, including a front porch that seats as many people as other entire tea rooms. You might think it would feel more like a restaurant, but the tea-room feeling remains throughout, because Catherine Van Dyke has made each room feel like a separate entity. I sat in the spacious garden room, where wrought-iron furniture, a stone floor, a wall stencilled with holly-hocks and wooden bird houses, and hanging vines and latticework all help to bring the outside indoors. The other rooms are decorated in an old-fashioned, elegant country style. The house itself was built in 1832 and was fully renovated six years ago when the Van Dykes purchased it.

Catherine's menu offers a reasonably priced and extensive selection of homemade savouries such as Scotch pies, chicken pot pies, sandwiches, salads and desserts. Afternoon tea and scones, served

with preserves, marmalade and cream, is about $4 per person. The menu changes seasonally.

🫖 TEAS SERVED: Irish Breakfast, Monk's Blend, Jasmine. Fruit and herbal infusions are also available.

Dishington's Tea Room

Jan Cottle, owner
28 Main Street East, Lambeth
519-652-2818

Monday through Saturday 10 to 4, Sunday 12 to 4.
Wheelchair accessible.

To get to the tea room, you pass through a gift shop whose walls and shelves are attractively stocked with dried flowers and wreaths, assorted giftware and a good selection of loose teas.

This is a pretty and cosy tea room — boughs and wreaths of dried flowers on the walls, rich pink, dark green and blue floral tablecloths and balloon valances, pink upholstered chairs and tiny floral wallpaper provide an abundance of colour and pattern that works beautifully. The artwork on the walls, mostly Canadian cottage and country scenes, is all for sale, and even the mirror, shelf and knickknacks in the ladies washroom are for sale.

The menu offers dishes to suit all tastes, all times of the year and all weathers. You may choose to tuck into a spinach salad with nuts and mandarin oranges, a salmon quiche, a steak and kidney pie, or a vegetarian lasagna, or enjoy an old-fashioned tea for two. A trolley laden with home-baked desserts will tempt you with the likes of bumbleberry pie, brownie sundae, praline cheesecake and lemon cake. Try to resist the three-storey carrot cake, very moist, full of raisins, topped with cream cheese icing and coconut. Apparently it

takes two days to make, but not nearly that long to eat. The china the food was served on was exquisite — the dishes looked like delicate white petals. (It was Coalport bone china Countryware; I was so taken with the pattern that I looked for the name on the bottom of my teacup while it was still half full.)

Every little detail was attended to in this tea room and was delightful. I highly recommend it. Lunch for two came to under $20.

TEAS SERVED: Formosa Oolong, Darjeeling, English Breakfast, Earl Grey, Market Spice, and Japanese green tea. Herbal and fruit infusions also available.

LOCAL INTEREST: Visit nearby London for the excellent Children's Museum, the University of Western Ontario, and the London Art Gallery.

The Great British Emporium Tea Room

Judy Luft, owner
169 Front Street, New Dundee
519–696–2223

Tuesday through Saturday 10 to 5, Sundays and holiday Mondays 11 to 5. Open for dinner Friday and Saturday evening, winter months only.

Enter the front doors of this fascinating emporium and you are transported back in time to the end of the nineteenth century. The general store, built in 1887, today sells a variety of British goods as well as antiques and curious oddities. The drawers of the original wooden cupboards hold bills of sale from the first store. Chocolates are made on the premises — proof was the aroma in the air. You may find it difficult to tear yourself away from the shop, with so much to look at, but carry on into the cosy tea room at the back, where the country-store feeling continues with pine wainscotting, bright tablecloths and old

wooden chairs, and interesting memorabilia on the walls.

The menu has a British, yet eclectic, theme. Spoil yourself with a traditional Scottish cream tea, or with crumpets and "real British" Typhoo tea. For heartier appetites, try the ploughman's lunch, or the country pâté, flavoured with herbs and sherry and served with Scottish oatcakes, or a seafood savoury — a shrimp and crab salad topped with Swiss cheese broiled on oatmeal toast, and served with fresh fruit. Whatever you order, be sure to enjoy the scrumptious homemade oatmeal bread. Desserts are a delight here, from the famous rhubarb–raspberry pie served with Devon cream to the two wheat-free specials, chocolate cake and shortbread.

LOCAL INTEREST: Follow scenic paths along Alder Creek, which pours into the Nith River, or visit Castle Kilbride in nearby Baden.

Afton's Tea Room and Gifts

Joanne Cantor, owner
1068 Hyde Park Road, Hyde Park, London
519-641-3041

Monday through Saturday 9:30 to 4:30. Wheelchair accessible (ramp).

This family-run tea room welcomes you with sun–filled paned windows framed by light, lacy balloon curtains. Simple, well-chosen furnishings and pretty, antique china lend a Victorian air to the room. It is a large room, but has a delightful bright decor and only eight tables, so there is definitely a feeling of comfort and spacious-ness here. It is quiet enough that you can talk to your tablemates or eavesdrop, whatever mood you're in.

The food is all homemade and includes luncheon items such as homemade soups, salads, snow crab on a croissant, and steak and

mushroom pie, absolutely packed with deliciously tender cuts of steak. "Decadent Indulgences" listed on the chalkboard included chocolate raspberry truffle cake — a dense chocolate cake with a raspberry kick, quite reminiscent of tartufo — carrot cake, and chocolate almond cheesecake. All the baking is done by Joanne Cantor's daughter, Melissa. The food was absolutely top-notch, and lunch for two, including one dessert, came to under $20.

TEAS SERVED: Earl Grey, English Breakfast and Orange Pekoe. Herbal teas and flavoured teas are also available.

LOCAL INTEREST: There are many antique stores in the area, right on Highway 22. The quilter's supply shop next door attracts customers from all over Ontario.

The McKie House

Giselle St. John, owner
4 Albert Street (on Highway 97), Plattsville
519–684–7667

Wednesday through Friday 11 to 4, Saturday and Sunday 11 to 5:30.

Giselle St. John and her husband, Joe, moved eight years ago from Toronto to Plattsville to this beautiful Victorian home, originally built in 1904. Giselle began by selling crafts in her home, gradually adding a few tables, and that venture evolved into the lovely tea room it is today. Locals love the friendly atmosphere, and it is a haven for tourists. There is a feeling of spaciousness, warmth and comfort, and Giselle chats easily to her customers, making everyone feel equally welcome. This is a delightful spot — definitely one of my favourites.

Personal service, home cooking and value for money are the most important ingredients at McKie House. Everything is freshly prepared

in the kitchen, including the breads. Check the blackboard, as every day brings a new special. Sandwiches, quiches served with salad, and soups are daily standards. Tuck into the house favourite dessert, cream pie with raspberry puree, or go for the traditional cream tea, which is perfect, with two warm scones, Devon cream, preserves and tea for only about $4. Come summer, what could be nicer than taking tea on the large wraparound front porch?

LOCAL INTEREST: Castle Kilbride, built in 1877 by James Livingston and named after his birthplace in Scotland, is fifteen minutes away in Baden. In Washington, five minutes away from Plattsville, visit the Brethern farm, a community farm of Hudderites who sell goose–down comforters, slippers and winter coats.

The Gingerbread House

Lynn Van Wyck, owner
19 St. Andrew Street, Port Dover
519–583–0249

Wednesday through Sunday 11 to 8. Reservations suggested on weekends. Wheelchair accessible, including washrooms.

The lovely pale yellow house, one block from the beach of Lake Erie, is really two houses in one. The original is an old sea captain's house dating from 1870 that was jacked up and added to in 1909.

Lynn Van Wyck, who, with her husband, Peter, owns the tea room and bakery, is happy to tell the history of their business. They started in 1984 as Sun Country Farm Market in Smithville, Ontario. It wasn't long before the sales of home–baked squares, muffins and cookies outperformed the fruit and veggies. In 1988 they opened at the present location, initially as a bakery. After customers started asking for a place to sit down with a cup of tea to consume their

bakery purchases on the spot, the first five tables were set up, and in 1990 a tea room was established. By continuously listening to their customers, this is the little tea room that continues to grow in size and success.

The atmosphere is serene. Classical music plays softly; local artwork graces the walls; stained-glass table lamps, designed by a local artisan to match Lynn's china, illuminate each table. The Gingerbread House is a favourite with locals — from the bridge club regulars to the highschoolers who participate in the gingerbread house contest every December.

The menu reads like a mission statement, guaranteeing customers the highest quality fresh ingredients, locally produced if at all possible and unadulterated by additives or preservatives, plus baked goods from old-fashioned recipes. You'll even find a list of ingredients used in the dishes on the back of the tea room menu. The Van Wycks also make an effort to use local products that emphasize a Canadian identity, as in the Canadian Buffalo soup, served with cheddar crackers homemade with seven-year-old cheddar.

It wouldn't have done to leave without tasting the Gingerbread's signature dessert — a dome-shaped gingerbread cake with crème fraîche; the taste is much anticipated, as the lovely fragrance is enticing. And it wouldn't do to leave without a box of decorated gingerbread people or some of the twelve kinds of cookies — perfect for dunking in your cuppa when you get home — including gingersnaps, old-fashioned sugar cookies, lemon squares and brownies. Lynn makes mountains of Christmas shortbread during December, and there is always orange cake served with crème fraîche, brandy snaps filled with whipped cream cheese and candied ginger, Georgian pecan cake served with whipped cream, or chocolate torte with cherry sauce. Light delicate crêpes are dusted with powdered sugar and covered

with a generous spread of luscious, wild blueberries. All of these are warm, comforting desserts, especially with a big pot for two of quality tea, brewed the proper way, with loose leaves and a strainer. Lynn says she refuses to let a tea bag inside the door.

TEAS SERVED: Darjeeling, Nilgiri, Assam, Ginger and Cardamon.

LOCAL INTEREST: Check out the Lighthouse Festival Summer Theatre, or try your luck fishing for perch and pickerel on Lake Erie.

Old School House Tea Room

Gary and Eileen Carr, owners
131 Talbot Road, Highway 3, Shedden
519-764-2272

Tuesday through Sunday 10 to 4:30, Sunday brunch 10:30 to 2:30, closed Monday. Closed from Christmas Eve to the first Tuesday in February.

This building, constructed in 1866 for $1,000, was the schoolhouse for the village and surrounding area for a hundred years. In 1984, Gary and Eileen Carr devoted themselves to restoring and retaining as much as possible of the original structure before opening their tea room that same year.

Nancy Smith, who does all the excellent baking for the tea room, attended school here from grades one to eight, as did her mother and grandmother before her. The tea room is a large, open space with a kitchen off to one side. The original Gothic windows with stained glass in the arches are breathtaking.

Brunches on Sundays are well attended. The menu is simple — soups, salads and sandwiches — but portions are substantial. Nancy will tell you to save room for pie — coconut cream, cherry, blueberry

or raisin. Or go local with rhubarb custard or rhubarb crisp. Lunch for two with dessert is about $16.

 TEAS SERVED: Darjeeling, Earl Grey, Orange Pekoe. Fruit teas are also available.

LOCAL INTEREST: Shedden is known as the Rhubarb Capital of Ontario and celebrates its claim to fame annually the second weekend in June with the Rhosy Rhubarb Days festival.

Nanny's Tea Room

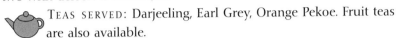

Eagleview Manor Bed and Breakfast
Pat and Bob Young, owners
178 Widder Street East, St. Mary's
519-284-1811

Tea by appointment only, at 24 hours' notice.
Small groups accommodated.

Eagleview Manor was built in 1905, and today serves as a popular retreat for Stratford Festival attendees. The house sits on top of a hill with a fabulous view over the town of St. Mary's. The entire house is breathtaking, from the huge winding staircase to each beautifully furnished B & B room.

Taking tea at Eagleview is like visiting good friends in their dining room. Tea is served in a comfortably elegant dining room; the original oak panelling and stained-glass windows remain and a small table sits in the bay window overlooking a pool. An antique walnut table and matching sideboard are graced by a gleaming silver tea service and antique silver flatware on white Battenberg lace.

A Victorian tea is served in the traditional manner. A triple-tiered serving dish arrives, heavy with tiny tea sandwiches, fresh fruit, and fabulous homemade scones, accompanied by strawberry preserves,

rhubarb preserves, lemon curd and Devon cream. All the food is superb. Prices ranges from about $4 for scones and tea to about $8 for the full Victorian tea.

Take a few friends, bring your quilting group, or honour someone's birthday here for a truly enjoyable outing.

LOCAL INTEREST: Snuggled in a beautiful valley at the confluence of the Thames River and Trout Creek, St. Mary's is a novel blend of Victorian charm styled in locally quarried limestone. Be sure to see St. Mary's Museum and the Fanshawe, Wildwood and Pittock Conservation Areas. The Opera House on Water Street is one of the most magnificent architectural accomplishments of nineteenth-century Ontario. Although it now houses apartments, it is a tribute to the stonemasons who built it.

Talbot Trail Tea Room

Wayne and Melody McKinnon, owners
86 Talbot Street, St. Thomas
519-633-8040

Tuesday through Friday 7:30 to 7:30, Saturday and Sunday 9 to 7:30, closed Monday.

The Talbot Trail Tea Room has an understated country decor, with ice-cream-parlour-style chairs, pine tables and pine floors, and lots of plants.

The menu is very extensive, and includes soups, salads, Lake Erie perch, quiches, stews, chili, and a huge selection of sandwiches. All desserts are baked on the premises, including pies, pralines and cream cheesecake, carrot cake and butter tarts.

This tea room was notable for the attention paid to the tea — our server mentioned that it would be a few minutes while the kettle

boiled, and made a point of telling us to let the tea steep. Milk was on the table, but it was suggested that we not use it for herbal tea. How refreshing to find tea-knowledgeable people serving. Wayne and Melody McKinnon rotate their staff through every job in the tea room, from dishwashing to cooking to serving. The success of this unusual strategy is reflected in the competence and pleasant attitude of the staff.

Be sure to see the tea room's small-scale model of a 1920s circus, built over a fifteen-year period. "Ryckman Bros Miniature Circus" is complete with circus tents, elephants, audiences and three-ring acts, and takes up an entire side room.

LOCAL INTEREST: Directly across the street from the tea room is a full-size monument to Jumbo, the African elephant, star of the Barnum & Bailey Circus, who had a fatal collision with a Grand Trunk locomotive on his second visit to St. Thomas, in 1885.

Harry Ten Shilling

Roxanne Jervis, owner
9 Huron Road, Shakespeare
519-625-8333

January and February weekends only 11 to 4; March through December Tuesday through Sunday, phone for exact hours; July and August daily, call for hours.

It's not hard to imagine what Shakespeare looked like a hundred years ago, because even at first glimpse, one can see it wouldn't look much different than it does today. After a wander around the village, stop in at Harry Ten Shilling. Make your way through the little attached shops (a women's clothing store, a bookshop/card store, and a shop selling teas, English foods, and tea accessories), and you will find the tea room nestled among the trees at the back of the building. It is very

bright, with large picture windows and ceiling skylights, and incredibly spacious, but maintains an old–world charm with antique pine tables and chairs and a backdrop of cranberry floral wallpaper. That sunny day our table overlooked the trees and bird feeders kept quite busy by all the beautiful finches. The resident cat, Ginger, who is not allowed in the tea room, hovered under our table until the waitress left.

The accent is on traditional English food — savouries, scones, quiches, soups and delicious sandwich selections, and sweets — all prepared on the premises. Afternoon teas are a favourite here. We had the Shakespeare tea for two — pumpkin and lemon cranberry tea bread, as well as scones, butter, a choice of jams, Devon cream, and their house blend tea, Boston Harbour, which is a blend of Indian, Darjeeling and Ceylon. Tea is laid out very properly, with all the expected tea accoutrements. Teapots are topped up without asking, and only quality tea is served. A cheese scone tea consists of warm cheese scones, with apple, cheddar cheese and butter and Boston Harbour Tea. Sweet lovers will be tempted by such treats as Victorian chocolate mousse cake, Harry Ten Shilling cheesecake, and chocolate fantasy pie. Lunch for two is about $20.

TEAS SERVED: Boston Harbour, Earl Grey, and English Breakfast. Herbal and fruit teas are also available.

LOCAL INTEREST: Shakespeare's main street is lined on both sides with antique businesses, specializing in furniture and china. Nearby attractions include the Stratford Festival and Brickman's Botanical Gardens.

> Tea in the morning, tea in the evening, tea at supper time,
> You get tea when it's raining, tea when it's snowing.
> Tea when the weather's fine
> You get tea as a mid-day stimulant
> You get tea with your afternoon tea
> For any old ailment or disease
> For Christ sake have a cuppa tea.
>
> The Kinks (Ray Davies), "Have a Cuppa Tea"

Mrs. Carter's Tea Room

Laura and Tony Carter, owners
116 Downie Street, Stratford
519-271-9200

Monday through Thursday 11:30 to 5, Friday 11:30 to 9,
Saturday 11:30 to 8 and Sunday 11:30 to 3.

The quiet luxuriousness of moss-coloured walls and ceiling in this tea room gives it an elegance made cosy with a fireplace flanked by bookcases. It has rather a men's club feel to it, but welcomes all visitors with tables and Windsor chairs of dark wood, and comfortable floral wing chairs in dark greens and muted burgundies. The centerpiece on each table is cleverly done — it's a toppled-over teacup filled with dried flowers, dried apple and orange slices.

Tony and Laura Carter have pulled together a menu that is wonderfully expansive, with some new twists on standard tea room fare. Tempt yourself with a choice of uniquely divine chicken crêpes filled with ricotta cheese, sun-dried tomatoes, pine nuts and fresh basil in an incredible spinach pesto sauce, or traditional steak and vegetable Cornish pasties, or a "Ploughperson's" lunch that has assorted cheeses with apple chutney, chicken liver pâté, garlic pâté, fruit and a baguette. Each is served with a salad for about $8. Even the sandwiches offer a gourmet twist.

Carter tea for two includes deliciously light scones, sweets, Devon cream and preserves, and tea, while the high tea adds finger sandwiches to this list. The ambience and excellent food will be sure to bring you back again.

LOCAL INTEREST: Stratford offers much to see and do — besides the plays at the Stratford Festival, there are dozens of antique shops, as well as lovely picnic sites and tour boats along the Avon River.

Palmer and Hunt's Tea Room

Karen Hunt, owner
89B Downey Street, Stratford
519–273–4392

Theatre season (May through October): Daily, hours vary, open late Saturday night. November through April: Monday through Saturday 11 to 4:30. Wheelchair accessible. Reservations required in theatre season only.

This tea room adjacent to the Avon Theatre is richly furnished and decorated, with dark pink walls, Battenberg lace, glass tabletops, hanging lamps, an original punched–tin ceiling and gleaming pine tables and chairs. A small gift section sells tea, teapots, mugs, tea cosies, tea gift–boxes, tea cards, jams and other tea paraphernalia.

Karen Hunt knows her tea and will not compromise on how it is served. She serves loose tea, with boiled water, heats the teapots, and lets her customers know that it will take a little bit of extra time.

The menu is very appropriate to a tea room, offering a good selection of sandwiches and a daily soup. Sandwiches are made with very thick, wonderful fresh bread. Cheesecakes and pies are always a temptation here.

A tea for two, high tea, power tea, and nursery tea are all available. The power tea is ideal for committee meetings (reservations required), and includes finger sandwiches, finger cakes, vegetable sticks and tea for about $7 per person. Tea for two gives you a choice of teas, two currant scones, preserves, Devon cream, shortbreads and chocolates. The nursery tea includes children's tutti–frutti tea, half a scone, one shortbread and a finger cake for about $3. What a delightful way to introduce children to the simple pleasure of having tea.

TEAS SERVED: Formosa Gunpowder, Japanese Sencha, Jasmine with flowers, Mousakellie (an organic tea), Monk's Blend, Estate Orange Pekoe, and Castleton Estate Second Flush Darjeeling. Many fruit and herbal infusions are also available.

The Village People Tea Room & Gift Shoppe

Diane Pearson, owner
242 King Street, Thorndale
519-461-0635

Sundays and Mondays 12 to 4, Tuesday through Saturday 10 to 5.
Closed Mondays in winter.

Step through the country gift shop to a bright and sunny tea room, a cottagey room with pink floral tablecloths to match the pink cushions on the white plastic chairs. This simple country tea room makes a good stop for a snack or lunch en route to London, Bayfield or Exeter. (The new-age background music — waves roaring and crashing — was a little intrusive.)

The menu features simple but substantial fare — soup, salad, cheese biscuits, salmon qiche, tuna melts, and chili. Sweets include carrot cake, triple crown lemon pie, raspberry swirl cheesecake, or scones and preserves.

Lunch for three was about $16.

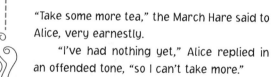 LOCAL INTEREST: Thorndale is only ten minutes from London. Look for the Fanshaw Conservation Area, the Thames River, and area orchards and greenhouses.

49

"Take some more tea," the March Hare said to Alice, very earnestly.

"I've had nothing yet," Alice replied in an offended tone, "so I can't take more."

Lewis Carroll,
Alice's Adventures in Wonderland

Jennifer's Tea Room

Linda Shank, owner
144 Dundas Street North, Woodstock
519–421–3464

Monday 11 to 2, Tuesday through Saturday 11 to 9.

This beautiful old house was a courthouse in its former life. It has a huge wraparound porch, and its rooms are light and spacious, with beautiful original pine floors still intact. The tea room is very simply decorated with wooden chairs and lace tablecloths.

Light lunch features soups, sandwiches, pasta dishes, quiches, crêpes, stir-fries, and a variety of salads. Afternoon tea offers scones with preserves, muffins or tea biscuits for about $2. You may choose to tuck into dessert crêpes with raspberries, peaches or mandarin oranges, or dip a fork into one of the many kinds of cheesecake, all baked on the premises — chocolate, raspberry swirl, cappucino, chocolate mint chip, plain cheesecake with fresh fruit or Bailey's, or strawberry swirl. Brownie cake and apple and blueberry crisp are also sure to please.

 TEAS SERVED: China Black, Darjeeling, Earl Grey, Jasmine, English Breakfast, and a selection of herbal and fruit infusions.

Tea had come as a deliverer to a land that called for deliverance; a land of beef and ale, of heavy eating and abundant drunkenness; of grey skies and harsh winds; of strong-nerved, stout-purposed, slow-thinking men and women. Above all, a land of sheltered homes and warm firesides — firesides that were waiting — waiting, for the bubbling kettle and the fragrant breath of tea.

Agnes Repplier, *To Think of Tea*

OTHER PLACES TO HAVE TEA IN THE LONDON REGION

The Little Country Cottage Tea Room, 25 Robison Street, Simcoe, 519–426–9990.

The Boston Tea Room, Concession 5, off Highway 24, south of Brantford, 519–443–8478, by appointment only.

The Cottage at Glenhyrst Gardens, west of Ava Road, north of Inwood Drive, Brantford, 519–756–5932. Lunch and afternoon tea from May to October.

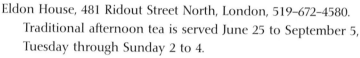

Hampstead's Tea Room, Arva, 519–660–8424.

Eldon House, 481 Ridout Street North, London, 519–672–4580. Traditional afternoon tea is served June 25 to September 5, Tuesday through Sunday 2 to 4.

By the Garden Gate, Brickman's Botanical Gardens, Wartburg, 519–393–6223. English tea room at the entrance to the gardens. Light lunches and teas served daily from 10 to 5.

Old Roses 'n' Tea, 698A Dundas Street, London, 519–645–7777.

Trifles Tea Room, 326 Main Street, Port Dover, 519–583–1313. High tea served daily from 2 to 4, for about $7.

At last the secret is out,
as it always must come in the end,
The delicious story is ripe to tell an intimate friend;
Over tea-cups and in the square the tongue has its desire;
Still waters run deep, my dear,
there's never smoke without fire.

W.H. Auden, "The Twelve Songs"

TimBri Tea Room

Tim and Bridget McElhone, owners
40 Eastern Avenue, Acton
519–853–5231

Monday through Friday 11 to 4, Saturday and Sunday 11 to 5.

This comfortable tea room decorated in pale pinks and navy is lit by bright, sunny windows and pink Tiffany lamps.

Choose from an imaginative selection of soups, quiches and sandwiches as well as daily specials such as linguini with chicken and fresh vegetables, topped with feta cheese and served with garlic bread. Don't skip desserts; you can have bread pudding with warm rum sauce, or the incredibly sweet, warm caramel apple (a Granny Smith apple on shortbread crust with caramel and toffee puddles), or Snickers cheesecake, chocolate raspberry truffle, or bumbleberry pie.

The TimBri Tea for two, served on a three–tier plate, includes a selection of tea sandwiches, a rainbow of fruits and veggies surrounding a cool creamy dip, and an assortment of sweets, for about $15.

LOCAL INTEREST: Be sure to visit Wetherby's, around the corner from the tea room on Church Street — a captivating shop filled to the brim with authentic British food, toys, books and gifts, including Coronation Street collectibles. Or visit the Olde Hide House, known for its complete range of leather goods.

Belfountain Inn

Gwen Dumer, owner
792 Forks of the Credit Road, Belfountain
519–927–9219

Open for lunch and afternoon tea every day, dinner served
Wednesday through Saturday.

The Belfountain Inn provides a welcome respite after a hike through the neighbouring Forks of the Credit Conservation Area or fly-fishing on the Credit River. The colonial-style decor — barn-red board-and-batten walls, wood floors, gleaming pine tables and woven placemats — is soothing and refreshing. There are fresh flowers and small lamps on each table, and wonderful period light-fixtures.

The sweet smell of baking when you enter this delightful inn is heavenly. All the baking is done on the premises by Gwen Dumers. The menu offers a variety of sandwiches on a pita or whole-wheat bread, salads, Oktoberfest or spiced sausage, and fish and chips. Desserts change daily; offerings such as apple-berry crisp, strawberry-rhubarb crisp and apple bread, as well as delicious scones served with homemade preserves, make it difficult to choose just one. Lunch for two is under $20.

There is a huge addition overlooking the Credit River in the works. It will have a fireplace, massive paned windows and French doors that open up to a fabulous view.

Mad River Tea House

Linda Hill, owner
2 Francais Street, Creemore
705–466–3526

Monday through Saturday 11 to 5, Sunday 12 to 5. Open Easter
weekend, closed Christmas Eve. Wheelchair accessible.

This purple and yellow house right on the main street of Creemore
has a large front porch that holds several yellow iron garden
tables and chairs for those who want to enjoy their tea outside. No
matter the weather, someone will be sitting outside!

The Mad Hatter theme reigns supreme in this teapot collector's
haven. The walls and ceiling of this tiny tea house are decked with
hanging wire baskets holding tea balls, tea mugs and oodles of tea
necessities, tea ware, tea accessories — and tea. There are dozens of
teapots; turn around and you'll see dozens more, in every shape
imaginable — novelty teapots, traditional Blue Willow, Staffordshire,
and miniature teapot sets, some in miniature picnic baskets.

Jazz music playing softly adds a funky touch to the whimsical
atmosphere. You can feel the enjoyment that Linda Hill gets out of
this tea room, as it is so obvious how much effort she puts into it.

Light lunches include pasta salads, fresh croissants, veggies, pita
sandwiches and green salads. But if you just want a cup of tea and
something sweet, there is a wide selection of luscious cakes and goodies that come warm from the oven. Try a slice of carrot cake, a lemon
poppyseed biscotti, almond chocolate biscotti, or the fabulous blueberry scones with homemade preserves. Lunch for two, sharing a
dessert, was about $20.

LOCAL INTEREST: The Mad River is well known for fishing,
and beer lovers will recognize the town as the home of
Creemore Ale.

Leyanders Tea Room

Pauline Neufeld, owner
40–42 Mill Street, Elora
519–846–2756

Monday open for lunch only, Tuesday through Thursday 10 to 5,
Friday and Saturday 10 to 9. Wheelchair accessible.

Leyanders is on the main street of Elora and is probably one of its most important tourist attractions. As you walk through the rustic tea room, you are bound to be tempted by the appetizing pastries just inside the entrance to the espresso bar (Sweet Tooth and Thyme) attached to the tea room. Everything is made on the premises from recipes developed in their own kitchen; it's hard to decide what to choose. On the savoury side, there is a soup of the day, mushroom and cheese quiche, or chicken in a subtle red–pepper sauce, all served with home–baked bread and green salad, or a fresh tomato and feta salad, or a choice of sandwiches. Dessert delights to choose from included banana crêpes with chocolate, apple–berry crumble pie the way it should be — a generous portion and baked in a light flaky pastry — and an assortment of cakes.

For afternoon tea, you can indulge in cream tea, served with raisin or oat scones, clotted cream and strawberry preserves, or high tea, which includes a fresh fruit salad followed by scones, clotted cream and preserves, followed by a selection of finger sandwiches completed with dainty sweets, all accompanied by tea.

Once you have made your decision, sit back and enjoy the fabulous view, if you have been lucky enough to get a table by the window overlooking the Grand River. Lunch for two with two desserts was about $30.

TEAS SERVED: Earl Grey, Darjeeling, and Jasmine. Fruit and herbal infusions are also available.

Stonecroft Inn

Janet Robart–Morgan, Lynn Sholomicki, Margaret Reveley, owners
5331 Trafalgar Road, Erin
519–833–0778 or 519–833–0922

Thursday through Sunday 12 to 4.

This fabulous 1859 stone house, set way back in from the road and surrounded by trees, makes a most tranquil setting for a tea room. The tea room is part of a bed and breakfast run by two sisters, Janet and Lynn, and their mother, Margaret. The joint venture works incredibly well, as Janet's passions are decorating and gardening, while the baking and cooking are shared by Lynn and Margaret. The original exterior of the stone house serves as a fabulous interior stone wall in the tea room. Huge banks of windows line the other walls of the tea room, letting light in to all the tables. Terraced gardens beyond lead to two ponds stocked with trout.

The table settings are lovely, with pale green, peach and yellow table linens, and pretty white porcelain dishes. The creative ideas on the menu are equally appealing. Sandwiches are made on thick homemade bread. Soups of the day were basil and spinach with lemon cream, and minestrone al pesto, accompanied by slabs of the fabulous bread in silver baskets. A garden salad with raspberry balsamic vinaigrette was fresh and colourful. Scones are a visual treat — served and decorated with fresh strawberries. The Stonecroft Special Tea, for about $9 per person, includes sandwiches, savouries, pickles, scones with fresh cream, homemade preserves and dainties, presented on the tra–

ditional three-tiered tea server, with your choice of tea. The decor, food, and personal service all show a meticulous attention to detail.

You will visit for the charming country location, but you will want to return for the delicious, mouth-watering food and the hospitality of Janet, Lynn and Margaret.

LOCAL INTEREST: This is close to the Forks of the Credit Provincial Park and the Credit River. The nearby towns of Erin, Belfountain and Terra Cotta are good for browsing and antiquing.

The Ivy House Tea Room

Angela Dadd, owner
115 Main Street South, Georgetown
905-873-2754

Monday through Friday 9 to 4, Saturday 9 to 5, closed Sunday.
Wheelchair accessible. Reservations required for large groups only.

Georgetown is one of those towns that just would not be complete without a tea shop, and the Ivy House, set on the main street in a gracious old stone house, provides the perfect venue for a traditional teatime.

The pretty tables, set with fuschia tablecloths, fresh flowers and crisp white Royal Doulton china, and the fascinating stream of customers make this a very special place to visit for lunch or tea. The busy atmosphere of the tea room was handled with grace and finesse by the staff.

The Ivy House menu offers an incredible range of sandwiches, vegetarian dishes, a daily soup, an asparagus and two-cheddar quiche and a ploughman's lunch with cheeses, pickled onion, Branston relish, egg and a roll. At teatime, traditional scones with Devon cream and strawberry preserves are available. But if you crave something

sweeter, there is also crème caramel or chocolate raspberry tartufo. Angela Dadd's mother does all the baking; the scones were light, moist and creamy, definitely among the best I've tasted.

Mr. McGregor's House Tea Room

Judy Craik, owner
10503 Islington Avenue, Kleinburg
905–893–2508

Daily 10 to 6.

Look in the tiny village of Kleinburg for Mr. McGregor's House, a white frame cottage that is home to the world of author Beatrix Potter, whose stories have delighted adults as well as children since the turn of the century. Step into the Peter Rabbit Room, where you'll discover gifts galore, including baked goods, jams, chutneys, maple syrup and, of course, a great selection of Beatrix Potter and Peter Rabbit gear.

The tea room is tastefully decorated with Canadian antiques. This is a self-serve tea room, with salads, quiches and meat pies to choose from, and cider, coffee, and a mouth-watering display of desserts laid out on the centre tables. There are no obvious signs directing you to serve yourself, so I had to find a server to ask how to get a cup of tea, which was a bit awkward. I must admit that I like to be served when I go out for tea, but this did not really detract from the delicious array of foods or the pleasant setting.

Tea. Earl Grey. Hot.
Jean Luc Picard, *Star Trek*

Carrot cake, oat squares, shortbreads, scones with cream and jam, chocolate mousse cake, almond fingers and lemon tarts are just a sampling of the homemade sweets offered. Step outside for lunch or tea in the garden, which is graced with a huge spreading maple tree, and inhabited by Peter Rabbit, Jeremy Fisher, and other characters. On your way out, "confess," and you will be charged only for what you ate. Boxes and bags are available so you can take your favourites home. Lunch for two with tea and one dessert was about $16.

LOCAL INTEREST: The renowned McMichael Canadian Art Gallery draws visitors to Kleinburg year-round.

The Incidental Shop

Helen and Jim Ewing, owners
468 Queen Street, Paisley
519-353-5030

Daily 10:30 to 4, closed Sunday and Monday.
Closed New Year's Day to April 30.

First you must make your way through a captivating shop filled with antiques and collectibles to get to the tea room, which once housed a machine shop for the *Paisley Gazette*. Helen Ewing says the gift shop opened first, and she didn't believe the back room could be turned into anything useable. But Jim put his skills to work, first cleaning out the room and refinishing the original pine floors. He then renovated an enormous built-in cupboard into a showcase for Victorian caboodle, stripped and refinished the beautiful fireplace mantel, and built an unusual mirror that wraps around a curved wall and opens up the room so much that you don't notice the lack of windows. Once Jim and Helen were done decorating and furnishing

the room in rich hues of burgundy and dark green, the cluttered machine shop was transformed into a warm, elegant tea room.

The menu offers a wide range of sandwiches, homemade soups, chili, lasagna, quiches, and a cheese-and-cracker tray. For teatime treats, there are apple dumplings with cinnamon sauce and whipping cream, gateau basque with berry sauce, butter tarts, tea biscuits and cinnamon buns, and there are always two cheesecakes. Lunch for two with a dessert is about $23.

LOCAL INTEREST: The Saugeen River is good for canoeing and fishing.

Back Door Tea Room

Diane Bald, owner
Bright Ideas Gift Shop, 153 Main Street, Penetanguishene
705-549-6803

Daily 10 to 5, closed Sunday.

This bright, simply decorated tea room is at the back of Bright Ideas Gift Shop, which specializes in gift baskets, chocolates, gourmet food, and baby gifts. Do take time to have a good look through the shop.

The tea room's daily menu features soup, salads, sandwiches, frozen yogurt, muffins and cheesecake. Tea is served in antique cups and saucers, and you are encouraged to choose one that you like from the shelves. A huge selection of quality teas are available, many of them loose. This delightfully casual tea room is a favourite with locals and tourists alike.

LOCAL INTEREST: The Georgian Bay islands, the beach resorts on Nottawasaga Bay, and Sainte-Marie Among the Hurons are all nearby attractions.

Sheena's Kitchen

Sheena Henderson, owner
The Old Feed Mill, 357 Main Street, Schomberg

Daily 10 to 5:30. Closed Mondays January through March.

The feed mill in Schomberg was built in 1884, but was converted to shops only four years ago. It still has the original wood floors and feed mill chutes. This spot is a perfect daytrip destination; enjoy a country drive and lunch out, and then a browse through the shops in the rest of the mill.

Exposed rafters, stencilled walls, wood floors, calico tablecloths, and a hodgepodge of antique chairs make this tea room a simple country delight, perfect in the setting of the Old Feed Mill. An antique pine counter serves to display desserts, and antique pine cupboards hold the teapots.

Sheena Henderson has many regular customers, and no wonder. All the baking is done on the premises. Scones with jam and Devon cream were absolute perfection. Specials are listed on the blackboard and include such choices as vegetable soup and a scone, ham and potato bake, steak and mushroom pie, and manicotti. The selection of desserts — butter tarts, pecan tarts, carrot cake, apple and raspberry crisp and fruit pies — offers something for every sweet tooth. There is a separate list of take-home goodies.

Take time to wander through the shops beside the tea room. They are well-stocked with country accessories, furnishings, folk art, and seasonal and garden goods. Don't miss the bargain room at the back, where you will find unusual antiques and seconds. There is so much to look at here, you may have to be dragged out, as I was. But for now, the Old Feed Mill in Schomberg is a well-kept secret.

McGregor House

Anne and Jan Riddall, owners
123 Leeder Lane, Southampton
519–797–1702

Wednesday through Saturday 11 to 5, Sunday 12 to 5. Closed Christmas
until spring.

Just one street over from the main street of Southampton, this heritage home was built in 1875 by Peter McGregor, a local shoe-
maker. He and his wife, Elizabeth, raised eight children in this house.
The front porch spanning the width of the house is truly inviting,
with large wicker rocking chairs, colourful morning glories wound
around the porch columns, and below it, a garden all in hues of pink.

The sense of welcome and serenity is carried through into the tea
room itself, as does the pink colour scheme. Reproduction press-back
chairs fit in beautifully with the original pine floor. The ceilings are
high; windows are tall, lace framed, and sun filled. The burgundy wall
border has a tea motif. Tables are topped with ecru crocheted lace
over dusty pink, over floor-length ecru cloth, and are brightened with
fresh flowers, all in pink, of course.

Menu specials — soups, sandwiches, quiches and salads — are
listed on the blackboard. What a pleasure, to relax on the delightful
front porch and tuck into one of Anne Riddall's yummy desserts.
There's a Queen Elizabeth cake, raspberry trifle, or peach mousse in a
chocolate cup. Or you could indulge in a traditional cream tea with
scones, homemade preserves, lemon curd and Devon cream for about
$4. Afternoon tea for two comes with fancy sandwiches, scones, pre-
serves, lemon curd and Devon cream, goodies and tea for about $15.
It was nice to see a special children's tea on the menu, with fancy
sandwiches, goodies and a drink for about $3. Tea is served in antique
china, and only quality loose teas are served.

TEAS SERVED: Darjeeling, Nilgiri, Assam, and Japanese and Indian green teas. Flavoured and herbal teas are also available, including the McGregor House Tea, blended especially for the tea room.

Pine Plus Tea Room

Barbara Elliott, owner
201 Elm Street, Stayner
705-428-6538

Spring and fall, always open weekends and holidays, weekdays by chance. June, July and August, daily 10 to 5, except Wednesday. Closed November to May 1.

This quaint, tiny tea room has seating for only seven people. It is part of an antique business specializing in mirrors, collectibles, coatracks, and Mennonite tables and chairs. Select country and antique furniture is also sold.

The tea room is open when the antique shop is open. Only desserts are offered, and the selection changes often. The day we were there, carrot cake, date squares and a tea loaf were being served with tea.

TEAS SERVED: Specialty teas are available as well as Orange Pekoe and Earl Grey.

LOCAL INTEREST: Wasaga Beach, and fishing in nearby Georgian Bay attract visitors to the area.

Samuel Johnson described himself as a shameless tea drinker who "with tea amuses the evening, with tea solaces the midnight, and with tea welcomes the morning." It was perfectly normal for him to drink sixteen cups in very quick succession.

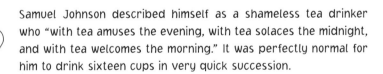

Mrs. Mitchell's

Maureen Baufeldt, owner
Highway 89, Violet Hill
519–925–3627

Tuesday through Friday 12 to 2, Saturday and Sunday 11 to 2. Also open
for dinner Tuesday through Sunday. Reservations required for dinner
but not for lunch or tea. Wheelchair accessible.

Maureen Baufeldt started out with a small cottage industry in her home, then moved her business into an old house twenty–three years ago, opening Granny Taught Us How, featuring country crafts and collectibles, stencilling materials, folk art and gourmet items. Sometime later Maureen also bought the old school–house next door, but it sat empty for a few years until her husband, a restoration specialist, set out to restore it to house the tea room. Renovations were soon so grand that she realized it had better be a restaurant instead of a tea room, so now it is a full–service licensed restaurant that serves afternoon tea.

Maureen has preserved the spirit of the school building and enhanced it with a simple country decor. There's a large main room and a smaller side room that has a huge wooden hearth laid with a gigantic dried–flower basket. Many of the regular customers in this converted schoolhouse are local people. Tourists who stop for tea after a country drive or a ramble on the Bruce Trail also appreciate the warm atmosphere and brisk service. As soon as you have asked for afternoon tea, baskets of sweet potato muffins and hot drop bis-cuits are brought to your table, as they are the only selections for teatime, along with tea, preserves, butter and sweet whipping cream, all for about $4 per person.

LOCAL INTEREST: Be sure to visit Maureen's store across the street, Granny Taught Us How. Nearby Hockley Valley offers Bruce Trail skiing and hiking.

OTHER PLACES TO HAVE TEA IN THE AREA FROM BRAMPTON TO LAKE HURON AND GEORGIAN BAY

Glen Cross Pottery and Tea Garden, Orangeville, beside the road entering the Hockley Resort, 519-941-6048.

Mountain Mist Tearoom, The Hockley Road, 5 kilometres east of Highway 10, Orangeville, 519-942-0145.

Hockley House Tea Room, The Driveshed, Hockley Village, Orangeville, 519-942-3130.

The Millcroft Inn, Alton, 1-800-383-3976. Afternoon tea is served daily on the terrace overlooking the millpond.

Chepstow Country Inn, Chepstow, 519-366-2274. Afternoon tea daily.

The Globe Restaurant, Highway 89, Rosemount, 705-435-6981.

McCrae House, 108 Water Street, Guelph, 519-836-1482. Afternoon tea in the garden every Wednesday in July and August. Reservations necessary.

Woodside Historical Site, Kitchener, 519-571-5684. Afternoon tea by the lily pond features a string quartet. Call for reservations and information.

Langdon Hall, Cambridge, 519-740-2100. Afternoon tea 3 to 5 daily at this fabulous country hotel with incredible gardens.

Princely Pear Tea Room, Queen Street Station, 9 Queen Street, Cookstown, 705-458-1055.

> So, hear it then, my Rennie dear,
> now hear it with a frown;
> You cannot make the tea so fast
> As I can gulp it down
> I therefore pray thee, Rennie dear,
> That thou wilt give it to me
> With cream and sugar softened well,
> Another dish of tea.
>
> Dr. Samuel Johnson (1709-1784), Untitled

Walker Hall Tea Room and Antiques

Dale Torch, owner
4927 Thirty Road North, Beamsville
905-563-5204

Monday through Thursday 10 to 3, Saturday and Sunday 11 to 5,
closed Friday.

This majestic home, completed in 1848, proudly displays ornate twelve-foot ceilings, four fireplaces, and formal living and dining rooms. It was built for the prominent Walker family, Loyalists who operated a successful shipping business on Lake Ontario after making the long journey up from North Carolina in 1776. Once the Walker family sold their properties, the Hall saw a progression of owners, and then Richard and Dale Torch purchased it in 1986.

Surrounded by 200-year-old oak and maple trees, and overlooking the shores of the lake, Walker Hall has been open as a tea room and antique store for four years. The entranceway and front room are filled with antique china and furnishings. Beyond this is a private dining room used for parties, weddings and business dinners. Walls are a rich candy-floss pink, offset by glossy white deep mouldings and trim. Wing chairs and a fireplace with a beautiful wood mantel make this an elegantly regal room, a lovely place for friends to gather.

The tea room looks as if several china cabinets were emptied out into it, as each wall is covered in china displays, all for sale. An open armoire is filled with antique china, all arranged in colour groupings of soft pinks and creamy greens. The room is cluttered beyond belief, but somehow the results are delightful.

Dale has a unique perspective on pricing the antiques and china. She doesn't want to make the prices formidable, and thinks that everyone should be able to afford at least one piece. So if a child is having afternoon tea out, and spots a teacup to buy as a surprise for mom or granny, it will only set her back a couple of dollars.

The orchard next door provides Dale with peaches, pears and plums for her pies, crêpes and crisps. Special dietary restrictions are catered to, but Dale does need to know ahead of time. Her soups contain no fat, and the menu lists many vegetarian items and also desserts that are low in sugar such as the peach raspberry crisp. Light lunches, homemade soups, croissant sandwiches, quiches and scones are all available.

LOCAL INTEREST: Beamsville is in the heart of the Niagara Fruit Belt, so in season, you'll want to stop at local stalls to pick up fabulous fruit and vegetables. Several antique shops are located near the tea room.

Taylor's Tea Room & Takeaway

Lorraine and Roger Stewart, owners
11 King Street West, Dundas
905–628–3768

Monday through Wednesday 10 to 4, Thursday through Saturday 10 to 9, Sunday 10 to 5. Reservations required.

Lorraine Stewart was raised in England and always visiting tea rooms, so running one comes naturally to her. In Taylor's Tea Room, strikingly decorated in dark green and pinks, with the original brick walls charmingly exposed, she has established a very popular place to share a cuppa with a friend. Two rooms accommodate tea room customers, and both of them were humming with locals and tourists.

The extensive menu leans toward English fare, and specializes in curries. Sandwiches include ham with Cheshire cheese; other dishes are shepherd's pie, steak and kidney pie, buck rarebit, crumpets, chips and even mushy peas! Curry sauces are made with their own curry powder, a special blend of twelve different spices. Of the several salads available, the rice curry salad, with shrimp, red and green peppers, peas, and mango chutney, is especially delicious. Or try a ploughman's lunch, which includes a wedge of bread, cheddar, Stilton, pâté, egg and sausage roll, pickled onions, and Branston pickle for about $10.

If you go for tea, you'll enjoy their special currant scones, baked fresh daily and served with homemade jam and real Devonshire cream. There is a minimum order during lunch of $7 per person. Taylor's is open for dinner three nights a week; on Friday nights, the special is roast beef and Yorkshire pudding.

LOCAL INTEREST: Dundas is a wonderful little town. Visit the Carnegie Gallery, originally the public library; Piccone's old-fashioned bakery, for baked goods to take home after tea; and Filedelphia, much more than an ordinary bookstore.

Sassafras Tea Room

Linda Mont, owner
1431 Pelham Street, Fonthill
905-892-1784

Daily 11 to 4, closed Mondays. Reservations for large groups only.

The decor of this tea room can best be described as funky, as is made apparent as soon as you are in the front entranceway by the tomato-red walls, the hall table covered in red and gold cloth, the gilt statue and gilt mirror. So many tea rooms depend on Victoriana

and country-style furnishings, making this brightly decorated tea room a refreshing change. Ice-cream-parlour chairs cluster round tables that sport bright plaid tablecloths and red napkins. The front picture window has teapots stencilled across it; the back window has a teapot frieze above it. There is a teapot clock, and the chalkboard menu is surrounded by teapot lights.

The menu offers soup specials (black bean and tomato or egg drop with lemon, for example), salads and sandwiches. Special sweets include their to-die-for bread pudding with whisky maple sauce, chocolate truffle wedge with raspberry coulis, or strawberry-rhubarb cobbler à la mode. Scones, served with real Devon cream and pre-serves, including quince, were beautifully presented and scrumptious. Linda Mont's emphasis on tea itself is welcome. Sassafras offers many loose teas, served in a cosied teapot to keep it hot longer, with a tea strainer and pretty antique cups and saucers.

My daughter and her friend, both nine years old, were made to feel very welcome. They were given a child's plate, a whimsical cabbage-style green plate bright with tiny food — cheese sticks, cucumber slices, baby carrots, celery, a cream dip in a tiny white con-tainer, miniature butter tarts, a mini muffin, and one delectable chocolate, all accompanied by pop or hot chocolate. This special treat completely captivated and delighted the kids. What a well thought-out addition to the menu — after all, the young ones may grow up to be tea room customers themselves. Lunch for four with two desserts was under $25.

This tea room is one of my favourites — for decor, atmosphere, delicious food, and the particular attention given to tea.

 TEAS SERVED: Earl Grey, Gunpowder and Lifeboat, as well as a choice of herbal and fruit infusions.

There is a subtle charm in the taste of tea which makes it irresistible and capable of idealization. It has not the arrogance of wine, the self-consciousness of coffee, nor the simpering innocence of cocoa.

Okakura Kakuzo, *The Book of Tea*

Eve's Eden

Evangeline Korpa, owner
89 Main Street West, Grimsby
905–945–0185

Tuesday through Sunday, 10 to 4, Thursday and Friday evenings 5 to 8.
Reservations suggested. Wheelchair accessible.

This building was originally a gas station, until Eve Korpa bought it in 1995. Eve found antique stained-glass windows, installed them in what was to become her tea room, and used the rich colours in the windows as inspiration for her decorating scheme throughout. Dark cranberry walls, cherry-wood chairs upholstered in dark green, and round tables covered with floor-length cloths, also in whites, cranberries and greens, pick up the window colours. Fresh flowers adorn each table. A piano in the corner awaits volunteers, who apparently do play when parties are in full swing. A second room, the Garden Room, overlooks an expanse of trees and has French doors opening out to a deck that accommodates more tables. Plans are underway to include a library room on the upper floor. The overall tone is one of comfortable elegance.

I ordered "only" a scone, which turned out to be a whole meal in itself — a buttery light scone served with fresh raspberry preserves with Devon cream piped on top and fresh raspberries sprinkled over. A blissful way to start a Sunday.

> They talk about Hitler's secret weapon, but what about England's secret weapon — tea.
> That's what keeps us going and that's what's going to carry us through the Army, the Navy, the Women's Institute — what keeps 'em together is tea!"
>
> A.A. Thompson

The menu also offers lunchtime temptations — soups, salads, phyllo pastries, and asparagus sandwiches. Be sure to inquire about the specials. Eve makes a point of serving seasonal vegetables and fruit from the area. Desserts available are strawberry or banana crêpes, treacle tart or carrot cake.

Prices are higher than in most tea rooms; two scones, one cinnamon bun, and three teas came to almost $20.

TEAS SERVED: English Breakfast, Earl Grey, as well as several estate teas, and herbal and fruit infusions.

Anchorage Tea Room

Bradley Museum
1620 Orr Road, Mississauga
905–822–4884

Sunday afternoons 2 to 4 only.

This Ontario Regency–style cottage on the grounds of the Bradley Museum was built in the 1830s and renovated in 1990. Volunteers served tea in the neighbouring barn to help raise money for the refurbishment of the cottage. The tea room is now run by volunteers who wear period costumes, delightfully proper navy-and-light-blue floor-length dresses, to serve a simple but traditional tea of scones with jam and cream, tea bread, homemade cookies, and tea, coffee or hot chocolate.

Original wood floors and lace over dark green tablecloths play up the navy-and-green floral wallpaper. The original enormous brick fireplace calls attention to the shelves beside it, which boast an interesting teapot collection.

Be sure to take a tour of Bradley House. Costumed interpreters plant and harvest crops, churn butter, and prepare hearty meals over

an open fire, recreating the simpler country life of a pioneer when families worked in harmony with each other and the seasons to live off the land. As their brochure says, this is a "piece of country in the heart of the city."

🔭 LOCAL INTEREST: Rattray Marsh Conservation Area, and Benares historic house, nearby on Clarkson Road North in Mississauga, are worth a visit.

Upstairs Downstairs Tea Room

Ellen Smyder, owner
88 Dunn Street, Oakville
905-338-1973

Monday 11:30 to 4, Tuesday through Saturday 11:30 to 5,
Sunday 12 to 5. Reservations required.

Your first impression upon entering this tea room will be of its elegance. It seems a tea room for the upper class, which suits the area in which it is located — an expensive neighbourhood swarming with socialites, children clad in private-school uniforms, and stores that cater to the well-to-do. But this is not a snobby tea room — it really is very friendly and accommodating to all customers, including children. It's a wonderful place to people-watch, a place to see and be seen, and I must admit to feeling underdressed and wishing I didn't have my winter boots on.

It also is one of the prettiest tea rooms, with forest green walls, bright, large-paned windows, and cushy club chairs pulled up to glass-topped tables.

The menu is very extensive, with unusual offerings such as almond croissant stuffed with shrimp and smoked salmon cream cheese sauce, and served with fresh greens, brie baked with pecans,

served with crispbread, angel hair pasta topped with cream sauce, and sliced cold breast of poached chicken with orange and papaya served with a light curried dressing. Crêpe choices were ham and asparagus, seafood or ratatouille.

This tea room is not for the gastronomically meek. If the lunch choices don't knock your socks off, the desserts will. The capuccino creme with meringue is too good to miss, but you could try the double white chocolate cake with strawberry filling, the four-fruit flan, the chocolate raspberry truffle cake, or the turtle fudge cake.

Afternoon tea, available from 3 to 4:30, includes finger sandwiches, scones with thick cream, preserves, sweets and tea for about $10. There is a minimum charge during lunch and during afternoon teatime. Between the comfortable seating and the delicious food, you may find it difficult to pry yourself away. The only minor flaw is that the tables are rather close together, but that wouldn't stop me from highly recommending it nor from returning.

TEAS SERVED: Gunpowder, Japanese green tea, Orange Pekoe, and Santos Estate. Herbal and fruit infusions were also available.

LOCAL INTEREST: There are loads of wonderful antique stores, secondhand shops, and walks along the Oakville lakeshore. Do visit the secondhand clothing stores — there are three of them, and they carry good-quality designer clothing at great prices.

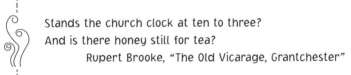

Stands the church clock at ten to three?
And is there honey still for tea?
Rupert Brooke, "The Old Vicarage, Grantchester"

Arabella's Tea Room

Port Colborne Historical and Marine Museum
61 Princess Street, Port Colborne
905–834–7604

June through September 2 to 4. Reservations for large groups only.
Wheelchair accessible.

This Edwardian–style tea room in the Williams Estate is part of the Port Colborne Historical and Marine Museum. Tea is served daily from June to September, but the tea room is also open at the beginning of December for the Christmas Festival, at which time they serve Christmas pudding with butterscotch sauce.

The tea room is run by eighty volunteers. Servers wear black, floor–length skirts, white blouses, and white aprons; the aprons are copies of one worn in 1915 by Mrs. George Murchie.

The tea room is housed in an enchanting clapboard house complete with a white picket fence, window boxes and flowering hedges. It has a feel of grandma's house to it, with a wooden screen door, white lace curtains, and floral wallpaper. The tea room was actually a cottage built in 1915 by the Williams family, and is named for Arabella Williams, born in 1865, who lived all her life in the house. Her grandparents were United Empire Loyalists and owned one of the farms crossed by Laura Secord in warning the British of the approach of the Americans in the War of 1812. Arabella died in 1950, a "spinster and owner of many properties." She deeded the block on which her residence stood to the Town of Port Colborne, on condition it was used for educational purposes. The new library opened on the property in 1957, followed by the Historical and Marine Museum in 1975.

Hot tea biscuits, homemade jams, and a choice of tea, coffee, lemonade or iced tea are available for about $3 per person.

The Mercantile Gift Shoppe and Tea Room

Rebecca Foster, owner
230 West Street, Port Colborne
905–834–5813

Monday through Saturday 11:30 to 4, Sundays open at 12.

Built in 1850, this unique building is Italianate in style, featuring a flat roof, rounded windows and a dominant cornice. Once through the delightful white-picket-fenced courtyard, you must pass through a temptingly stocked gift shop to the upstairs tea room. There the decor is all greens and pinks, very feminine and pretty. Pink cloths, large doilies and glass top the tables. Antique china cabinets are filled with teapots of all kinds. At one end of the tea room is a sitting area with a pink-striped floral couch and wing chairs, and beautiful pink Persian carpets.

A full afternoon tea includes scones, jams, tea sandwiches, madeleines, tea and cookies for about $10 per person. Tea was beautifully presented in traditional fashion on a three-tiered tray, with Royal Doulton china, lemon squeezers, sugar tongs, and cosied pots. A silver bell was placed in the centre of the table to ring for more hot water or scones — a lovely idea. My daughter ordered the Floral Fantasy, which came in a green glass pot-shaped dish and consisted of chocolate mousse on a layer of crushed Oreo cookies, topped with a spray of plastic pink posies. If you want to keep the flowers, the waitress will take them away, wipe them off (the stem is muddy from the chocolate "dirt"), and bring them back to you on a heart-shaped doily. What a delight for little girls.

Refreshingly, there is a no-tipping policy here; donations to a jar in the hallway are given to the Help a Child Smile Foundation. Last February, $2,000 was raised by this method.

The Lighthouse Tea Room

Wendy Mackie, owner
12 Lock Street, Port Dalhousie
905-937-4333

Tuesday through Sunday, closed January. Reservations encouraged.

We were fortunate enough to visit the picturesque village of Port Dalhousie on Music Festival Day. The village overlooks Lake Ontario and it was bustling with activity that day. Upstairs from the Murder and Mayhem Store, off Lock Street, is the Lighthouse Tea Room.

The tea room is quaint and cosy, with a country Laura Ashley style accomplished by white walls with blue trim and stencilled teapots and cups, and hanging baskets and dried flowers. The generous assortment of collectibles for tea lovers includes framed pictures, tea books, vinegars and preserves. There are actually three rooms, one a long galley–style windowed porch overlooking the street.

The menu offers standard tea room fare, including salads and soups. Among the "Sweets 'n' Treats" offered was "the best apple pie in Niagara," baked fresh daily — indeed the light flaky pastry was bursting with apples — and blueberry, strawberry, and apple–rhubarb pies. Lunch for two, sharing a dessert, was $15.

> Here's your arsenic dear.
> And your weed-killer biscuit.
> I've throttled your parakeet.
> I've spat in the vases.
> I've put cheese in the mouseholes. Here's your
> . . . nice tea, dear.
> Dylan Thomas (1914–1953), "Under Milkwood"

Robinson-Bray Tea Room

Rhonda Turner, owner
223 Queen Street South, Streetsville
905-542-7674

Monday through Friday 11 to 4:30, Saturday 11 to 5, Sunday 1 to 5.

This very elegant yet comfortable tea room, decorated in cream, with wood trim and lovely pleated cabbage-rose curtains, is situated in a classic redbrick Georgian house built in 1885 on the main street of Streetsville.

We were fortunate to visit on a Sunday in June when a Strawberry Garden Tea and Fashion Stroll was taking place. We sat on the side patio and were delighted with the menu, which, of course, had a special strawberry focus that day. For $10 per person, we were offered a strawberry soda, a medley of tea sandwiches, scones with Devon cream and strawberry preserves, a selection of hot and iced teas, and finally, a strawberry yogurt cake roll with a garnish of jewelled strawberries.

Rhonda Turner holds special theme teas monthly, including an August moonlight tea under the stars, a September back-to-school tea with an Alice in Wonderland theme for children, and teas at Thanksgiving, Mother's Day and Easter. She also teaches floral classes that include tea and scones for participants. The regular menu offers soups, salads, quiches, vegetable lasagna, crêpes and beef pie.

 TEAS SERVED: Darjeeling, English Breakfast, Earl Grey, Assam, China Keemun, as well as herbal teas.

There are worlds out there where the sky is burning, and the sea's asleep, and the rivers dream. People made of smoke and cities made of song. Somewhere else the tea's getting cold.

The Doctor (Sylvester McCoy) in "Survival," *Doctor Who*

The Royal Tea Room

Kerri Shepherd, manager
The Royal York Hotel, 100 Front Street, Toronto
416–368–2511 Ext. 2446

Monday through Friday 12 to 5, Saturday and Sunday 2 to 5.

This most elegant and charming tea room, rich in old–world char-
acter, can be found in one of Toronto's oldest hotels. When the
Royal York Hotel opened in 1929, it was the largest building in the
British Empire, and since then it has hosted over 42 million guests,
including three generations of the Royal Family, under its landmark
green copper roof. The Royal York has been putting on afternoon teas
since the 1930s, when tea and sandwiches cost 40 cents. These tea
dances included a live band and attracted hundreds of young people
on weekends.

Today, a traditional tea is served in silver teapots by friendly waitresses in smart black uniforms with white aprons and white collars.
The elegance that characterizes the Royal York has been lavished on
this airy tea room with gold wall–sconces,
lattice on the walls, large potted plants,
hanging plants and a gazebo roof.

> Polly, put the kettle on,
> we'll all have tea.
> Charles Dickens
> (1812–1870),
> *Barnaby Rudge*

During the week, afternoon tea or a
luncheon buffet is available. On weekends, afternoon tea only is available, but
you will not go hungry with their tea —
"three sinfully delicious courses." It begins
with seasonal berries and toasted honey crumpets. Dainty sandwiches,
cream scones with jam and clotted cream, and pastries are served on
an elegant three-tiered tea stand. Traditionally, one eats from the bottom to the top, so sandwiches are on the bottom tier, scones — divinely
light — and clotted cream in the middle, and pastries at the top. Tea of
your choice is included in the price of less than $15 per person.

The Royal Tea Room provides an elegant escape from downtown shopping in Toronto, and a delightful way to start or end an afternoon at the theatre with friends.

TEAS SERVED: (bags) English Breakfast, Darjeeling, Earl Grey, China Black, Orange Pekoe, Japanese green tea, Chamomile; (loose) English Breakfast, Darjeeling Himalaya, Russian Earl Grey, Finest Earl Grey, Royal Ceylon, Orange Windsor, Golden Vanilla.

Royal Tea Room Scones

These authentic cream scones, created by the Royal York's executive chef, George McNeill, are heavenly light and simple to make.

2 c. all purpose flour
1/4 c. granulated sugar
2 tsp. baking powder
1/2 tsp. salt
1/4 c. cold butter
1/2 c. raisins (optional)
2 eggs
1/2 c. milk
Glaze:
1 egg, beaten
pinch salt

In a large bowl, combine flour, sugar, baking powder and salt. With pastry blender or fingertips, rub in butter until mixture resembles coarse crumbs. Stir in raisins (optional). Make a well in the centre of the flour mixture. In a small bowl, use a fork to beat eggs and milk until blended. Pour into well. Use fork to mix with quick, light strokes to make a soft, slightly sticky dough. Press dough into ball and knead gently on floured surface 10 times. Pat dough into 3/4-inch-thick circle. Cut out, using 2 1/2-inch floured round cutter. Place rounds on greased baking sheet. Brush tops of scones lightly with glaze, and bake in 425°F oven for 15 minutes or until golden.

Makes 12 scones. Serve with strawberry preserves, clotted cream and tea.

Pause Awhile Tea Room

Margaret and Jim Robertson, owners
31 Main Street South, Waterdown
1–905–689–4741

Monday through Wednesday 10 to 5, Thursday through Sunday 10 to 9.

Margaret Robertson treats all those who come to the Pause Awhile Tea Room like old friends. The tea room is pleasant with lovely floral wallpaper and tablecloths in peach tones, and shelves displaying a collection of novelty teapots and miniature furniture. Servers wear tartan uniforms, which is a nice touch.

In this calm, unhurried atmosphere you can sit back and indulge in a delicious sandwich, freshly baked scones, or a cake chosen from the tempting menu. Good service and value are important to Margaret, and her menu offers a very reasonably priced selection. The pretty cosied teapots are regularly topped up without your having to ask, and nothing is too much trouble for the owner or the servers.

A private room is available for banquets, meetings, small weddings and other special occasions.

 LOCAL INTEREST: You'll find many Victorian gift shops and antique stores, historical homes and B & Bs in the area, and also Westfield Heritage Village on Highway 8.

The Old philosopher is still among us in the brown coat with the metal buttons and the shirt which ought to be at the wash, blinking, puffing, rolling his head, drumming with his fingers, tearing his meat like a tiger, and swallowing his tea in oceans.

Thomas Babington Macauley, *Life of Johnson*

Surprisingly, there are no tea rooms in the Niagara Falls, Niagara-on-the-Lake area, but the following is a list of hotels and restaurants that offer afternoon tea.

Angel Inn, 224 Regent Street, Niagara-on-the-Lake, 905-468-3411.

Buttery Theatre Restaurant, 19 Queen Street, Niagara-on-the-Lake, 905-468-2564.

Oban Inn, 160 Front Street, Niagara-on-the-Lake, 905-468-2165. Afternoon tea is apparently served in the bar from 3 to 5 P.M., but may go by the wayside if they are busy.

Pillar & Post Inn, King and John Streets, Niagara-on-the-Lake, 905-468-2123.

The Kiely Inn & Restaurant, 209 Queen Street, Niagara-on-the-Lake, 905-468-4588. The Victorian tea promises a selection of finger sandwiches, small cakes, tarts and slices with tea. The Devonshire cream tea includes deliciously light scones, butter, preserves and Devon cream with tea. This inn was built in 1832 and maintains much of its original charm. We had tea on the patio overlooking the garden.

Old Bakery Restaurant, 59 Queen Street, Niagara-on-the-Lake, 905-468-7217. Full afternoon tea with sandwiches and desserts.

Upper Canada Cookery & Café, 65 Queen Street, Niagara-on-the-Lake, 905-468-0958. Afternoon tea includes scones, Devon cream and jams.

Queenston Heights Restaurant, Queenston, 905-262-4276. Afternoon tea comes with a view of the Niagara River.

> Tea! thou soft, sober, sage and venerable liquid: thou female tongue-running, smile-smoothing, heart-opening, wink-tippling cordial, to whose glorious insipidity I owe the happiest moment of my life, let me fall prostrate.
>
> Colley Cibber 1671-1757 "The Lady's Last Stake," Act I, Scene I

Once Upon a Time Tea
   Room, at the back of the
   Highland House gift
   shop, Highway 115 at
   Highway 20 East,
   Fonthill, 905–892–3993.
The Lasting Impressions Gift
   and Tea Room, 356
   Ridge Road, Ridgeway,
   905–894–2059.
Heather's Antiques, Collectibles and Tea Room, 3864 Main Street,
   Jordan, 905–562–3184.

> Twinkle, twinkle little bat
> How I wonder what you're at.
> Up above the world you fly,
> Like a tea-tray in the sky.
> Lewis Carroll, *Alice's Adventures in Wonderland*

PLACES TO HAVE TEA IN THE TORONTO AREA

The Christmas Shop and Tea Room, 10473 Islington Avenue,
   Kleinburg, 905–893–2066.
Unionville Café, Embassy Suites Hotel, 8500 Warden Avenue,
   Markham, 905–470–8500.
Four Seasons Hotel, Lobby Bar, 21 Avenue Road, Toronto,
   416–964–0411 Ext. 4740.
Tea Tasters Café, 372 Bay Street, Toronto, 416–777–9779.
The Oracle Tea Room, 596 St. Clair Street West, Toronto, 416–653–4648.
   Have a cup of tea and a full tea-leaf reading for $25.
Intercontinental Hotel, 220 Bloor Street West, Toronto, 416–960–5200.
King Edward Hotel, King Street East, Toronto, 416–863–9700.
Prince Hotel, 900 York Mills, North York, 416–964–6641.
Wickerhead Café, 1919 Queen Street East, Toronto. Known for their
   fabulous scones.
Tartan and Lace, 6237 Main Street, Stouffville, 905–642–8333.
An English Tea Room, 161 Winchester Road, Toronto, 416–961–9944.
The Burr House, 528 Carrville Road, Richmond Hill, 905–884–0327.
   May through September.

Farmer's Kitchen

Joyce Hall, owner
334 Simcoe Street, Beaverton
705–426–7950

Daily 9 to 5:30, closed Sunday.

Pink tablecloths on round tables with burgundy painted chairs, original hardwood floors, floral wallpaper, and light music add up to a pleasantly inviting tea room. There is a real country feeling here. The tea room is combined with a bulk food store but unfortunately not separate from it; a simple lattice divider would make the tea room more private.

Everything is served on antique china. The daily menu, written up on a large chalkboard, includes salads, sandwiches and "Goodies" — lemon poppyseed cake, cinnamon rolls, tea biscuits and muffins. Two can enjoy lunch for under $15.

8 3

A little tea, one leaf I did not steal. For guiltless blood sped I to God appeal. Put tea in one scale, human blood in t'other, And think what 'tis to slay a harmless brother.
Gravestone epitaph of an English tea smuggler,
Robert Trotman (1765)

Forget Me Not Tea Room and Gifts

Marilyn and Allister Fraser, owners
30 Ontario Street, Bracebridge
705–645–1653

Daily 11 to 4, closed Sunday.

This 128-year-old home boasts a tea room and a gift shop well stocked with many tea varieties and an abundance of their own private-label gourmet food products, including fabulous dressings, vinegars and jams. The tea room, situated at the back of the house, is bright in candy-floss pink, burgundy and green. Tables and chairs are a mix-and-match collection of antiques, and they are all for sale. Fortunately, Marilyn Fraser has a relationship with many antique stores in the area, so if she needs to refurbish in a hurry, she can.

A separate tea menu has a surprisingly huge selection of teas. One would think this would be a regular feature of tea rooms, and it should be, but unfortunately, others choose to focus only on decor, food or whatever.

The tea room chef, Gwen Holmes, has journeyed extensively throughout Canada and brings to the table the varied tastes and trends experienced in her travels. Presentation of the food is top-notch, as is the taste, well justifying this tea room's listing in *Where to Eat in Canada*. The luncheon menu blackboard lists daily specials — soups, salads, open-faced sandwiches or, for example, grilled cheese stuffed pasta tossed in Muskoka Sizzler (their own grilling oil) with spinach, grilled vegetables and shrimp. You can choose from several homemade desserts, perhaps four-berry crisp, petite chocolate cups with Devon custard and fresh berries, or chocolate blackberry trifle. Lunch for two was under $18.

TEAS SERVED: Darjeeling, Assam, Ceylon, English Breakfast, Irish Breakfast, Earl Grey, Formosa Gunpowder, and Japanese Sencha, plus a variety of herbal and fruit teas.

Ms Ellie's Bistro, Bakery and Tea Room

Ellie MacNeil and Rob Burroughs, owners
Rosedale, near Fenelon Falls
705–887–5320

Daily 8:30 to 7.

This combination gift shop, restaurant and bakery has a small tea room nestled at the back of the gift shop. Customers are often drawn into a communal conversation, as this fabulous pine–panelled tea room seats only eight. That Ellie and Rob are creative is obvious in their upscale gift shop, which sells beautiful crafts and furniture, and also in the way they have furnished this tiny tea room — the table bottoms are old sewing–machine treadles, the tops are huge furnace grates topped with recycled glass, and the chairs are a happy mix of antiques.

You can order from the restaurant menu in the tea room as well. The menu features apple dumplings with rum sauce, a variety of cheesecakes, seasonal pies and fruit flans.

8.5

Whenever I sit in a high chair
For breakfast or dinner or tea,
I try to pretend that it's my chair,
And that I am a baby of three.
A. A. Milne (1882–1956) *Nursery Chairs*,
"The Fourth Chair"

Scotsman Point Resort, Afternoon Tea Room

Andrea Childs, owner
Buckhorn Lake, Lakefield
705–657–8630

Daily 1 to 5 mid–May to mid–October. In spring and fall, call ahead.

The tea room at this large resort directly overlooks Buckhorn Lake, a superb lake for boating, fishing and swimming. Andrea Child's family has owned the resort at Scotsman Point since 1949, but it has changed some since this dynamic woman took over twenty–five years ago, when her parents retired. Andrea added the tea room and conference centre, and these days hosts special weekend retreats.

A tea room may be an unusual focus for a lakeside resort, but this one is as popular with guests, some of whom have been coming to Buckhorn every summer for forty years, as it is with the locals. Rustic pine panelling, caned chairs and dark green tablecloths give the tea room a cottagey ambience completely in keeping with the peaceful lakeview. A deck at the front of the room has additional tables for when the sun is shining.

All the baking is done on the premises. Afternoon tea, very reasonably priced, includes a muffin, oat scones and tea biscuits, fresh daily, with an assortment of homemade jams and jellies, and coffee, tea, lemonade or iced tea. Special desserts may include mango cheesecake or lemon chiffon pie. The housekeeping cottages are close enough to be sociable, but still removed enough to be private. Go for afternoon tea, and you may find you want to stay for the week.

LOCAL INTEREST: Fishing on Buckhorn Lake yields pickerel, muskie, and bass. Whetung Gallery on Curve Lake features Ojibway art, and the Gallery on the Lake in Buckhorn specializes in wildlife art.

Gambell's Antiques and Tea Room

Ron Gambell, owner
3 North Street (across from the bridge), Minden
705-286-1532

Daily 11 to 4, high tea at 4.

Often it is the case that the owners of the tea rooms stand out more than the tea room itself, but at Gambell's, both do. Ron Gambell is a delightfully knowledgeable and chatty former car salesman. Gambell's store, proclaimed Haliburton Highlands "Most Unusual Store," is the quintessential antique shop — absolutely brimming with antique furniture, lamps, oddities, eccentricities, jewellery and other collectibles. Take the time to browse through this unique collection, which includes a fabulous selection of antique brass light fixtures.

Overlooking the river in this gem of a building, tucked in among the antiques, is the tea room where everything is for sale. Salt shakers, dishes, chairs, tables, teapots — if you like what you are drinking your tea out of, or you have fallen for the chair you are sitting in, buy it! Hanging from the rafters overhead is a collection of baskets, kitchen strainers and kitchen utensils. The walls are an organized jumble of collectibles.

The tea room offers a light menu of soups, sandwiches, tea and scones, promising decadent desserts and daily specials. It was temporarily closed when we visited, so the menu details will have to wait until you discover them for yourself.

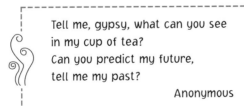

Tell me, gypsy, what can you see
in my cup of tea?
Can you predict my future,
tell me my past?

Anonymous

The Country Store and Tea Room

Eric Vogel, Leslie and Kathleen Ridgeway, owners
Belleville
613–962–0116

Monday through Thursday 8 A.M. to last call, Friday through Sunday
9 A.M. to last call.

The drive from Highway 62 by way of beautiful, rural Rednersville Road alongside Lake Ontario is a pretty one, reminiscent of the Niagara Parkway.

It is quickly obvious that this tea room is a tad unusual, as the hours listed say they are open until last call — 2 A.M. You may find yourself hesitating upon entering the Country Store and Tea Room. The front of the building is a country grocery store with a definite historical feeling — here is the local post office and movie rental store and there is a pool table and a video arcade game. In business for 200 years, this heritage establishment is the oldest continuously operating country store in Ontario.

At the back, through French doors, is a charming tea room and the local pub — the Bird and Beak — with original wood floors, pine tables and press-back chairs. Even though it is combined with a pub, it is every inch a tea room, boasting the largest selection of loose tea of any tea room I've been in so far. Even the owners admit that some days it is more of a tea room, and other days the pub takes over. The day I visited, it was a mix of patrons, and not a bad one. The advantage of pub hours for tea drinkers is that, if you wanted to, you could actually partake of tea, scones and Devon cream right up until last call.

The wonderfully large selection of teas is very refreshing, as very few tea rooms focus on tea and even fewer offer loose teas. This tea room has 38 choices, and if you like the one you choose, you can buy some to take home.

Solid nourishment runs to breakfast fare, soups and salads, and nachos, wings, burgers and pizza to appease the pub crowd. Assorted homemade fruit pies with ice cream, muffins and butter tarts are the dessert offerings.

Partaking of tea out of delicate antique cups and saucers, and indulging in incredibly delicious home-baked scones with the ever-important Devon cream and homemade strawberry jam while men at the adjacent table smoke cigarettes, swill beer and watch televised golf seems quite a paradox, but it's one that works beautifully in this setting.

Dutch Treat Tea Room

Cornelius White House Bed and Breakfast
Frank and Bonnie Evans, owners
8 Wellington Street, Bloomfield
613-393-2282

Saturday and Sunday 11:30 to 4. Closed Thanksgiving weekend until May 24. Wheelchair ramp. Reservations preferred but not necessary.

The Dutch Treat Tea Room and Cornelius White House B & B share space in a large Georgian-style redbrick house in this quintessential small Ontario town.

Frank and Bonnie Evans, owners and hosts, also make this their home. The house is filled with reproduction period furniture and antiques, paintings and decorative objects. Frank and his son added on the tea room three years ago, incorporating the exterior brick walls

of the house into the tea room. Beautiful multi-paned windows are topped with lace valances, and the trim throughout the tea room is painted in turn-of-the-century hues of sage green and burgundy. The atmosphere is warm, friendly and relaxed.

The menu is crammed with wonderful home-baked savouries, soups, sandwiches and salads, and sweets such as Belgian chocolate mousse cake, Cornelius White House Cake with fresh fruit and whipped cream, pies and even tapioca pudding. On balmy summer days, the side patio is an idyllic place to enjoy lunch, tea and dessert. Lunch for two with dessert is about $15.

Food for Thought Tea Room
& Book Shop

Pamela Slik, owner
Bloomfield
613-393-1423

Daily 11 to 4:30, except Sunday.

Smack dab in the middle of Prince Edward County, where the countryside is pure Ontario beauty, sits Food for Thought. Enchanting perennial gardens and wicker outdoor furniture spread out on the front lawn will draw you to the front door of this lovely house.

Thank God for tea! What would the world do without tea? How did it exist? I am glad I was not born before tea.

Sydney Smith, clergyman (1771-1845)

The decor is pink and green, with floral tablecloths and dishes, and pretty Tiffany lamps over each table. The music is classical; the art on the walls, some by Pamela's brother, some by other local artists, is decidedly funky and lends an upbeat tone to this delightful country tea room.

The food offerings are all homemade and change daily. Specials the day I visited were chilled gazpacho soup, chicken tarragon on romaine, chicken pot pie and pasta primavera salad. Desserts seem to be a priority here, starring raspberry pie, rhubarb sour cream pie and lemon poppyseed scones with preserves. Lunch for two is under $20.

On your way out, take a peek in the cosy reading room upstairs, which serves as a waiting room when all the tables are full. Book selections in the gift shop cover a range of interests — women's issues, spirituality, travel and cooking.

The Sap Bucket

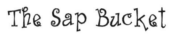

Diane Cocek, owner
Drummond Street, Smithfield, near Brighton
613-475-3636

Monday through Saturday 10 to 5, Sunday and holidays 12 to 5.

You'll find this small but cheerful tea room at the back of a Christmas store. Pink walls, forest green tablecloths, and wooden chairs make it pretty and cosy. Classical music plays in the background.

Menu choices are limited but quite adequate, and the food is delicious. Settle in with the special daily soup and a bagel sandwich. Desserts are all homemade, including strawberry–rhubarb, bumbleberry and lemon meringue pies, strawberry swirl cheesecake, and scrumptious butter tarts. Lunch for two with one dessert comes to about $13.

LOCAL INTEREST: This is a large apple-growing area — Highway 2 is known as the Apple Route. Applefest weekend is celebrated the last fall weekend in September. Presqu'ile Provincial Park, south of Brighton, is well known to bird-watchers, and by late August, thousands of migrating birds and Monarch butterflies can be seen there.

The Village Tea Room

Elaine Kempt, owner
1105 High Street, Keene
705-295-4566

Tuesday through Saturday 10 to 5, Sunday and holidays 11 to 5.
Closed January.

Keene is a lovely little village, with pretty, well-kept Victorian houses that all seem to have well-tended gardens. The tea room is located at the centre of Keene, and makes up one half of a country gift shop that is stocked from floor to ceiling. Waitresses wear floor-length gingham aprons and will direct you to choose from a black-board menu of tea selections and a "Today's Sweets" board.

Light lunches include chicken pot pie with salad, sandwiches and soups. Tea for two, which includes muffins, cheese and tea bread with tea, butter and jam, was about $7.

> Look here, Steward, if this is coffee, I want tea; but if this is tea, then I wish for coffee.
>
> *Punch*, 1902, vol. cxxiii

The Peppergrass Shoppe

July Caldwell, owner
2815 Princess Street, Kingston
613-634-7198

Monday through Saturday 10 to 4, closed Sunday. Reservations
are encouraged.

Although this tea room is situated in a strip mall, the country charm of the interior belies its location. Log-cabin–style pine walls, pine flooring, and pine tables and chairs cosy up the tea room, which brims over with country collectibles. The gift shop is temptingly filled with more treasures.

A wonderful selection of teas is offered, and if you can't make a decision, a portable "tea–sniffing station" will be brought to your table upon request, so you can see the teas and savour the aromas before ordering. Your waitress will describe the menu, as it varies daily. The day I visited, specials included creamy chicken tarragon crêpes with garden salad, broccoli and cheese quiches, and beef and mushroom turnover with homemade cauliflower soup and pan–fried potatoes. You can also order scones with Devon cream, lemon curd and fruit preserves. The mouth–watering scents of cinnamon rolls and carrot cake fill the air, as the baking is all done on site.

TEAS SERVED: Monk's Blend, Darjeeling, Oolong Orange Blossom, Earl Grey, Jasmine, and Ginger, along with several fruit and herb teas.

LOCAL INTEREST: There's lots to see and do in Kingston and area. Visit Fort Henry, take a ferry to Wolfe Island. Drive to Adolphustown and take the free ferry to Glenora, where you can see a lake on top of a mountain overlooking the Bay of Quinte with no apparent water connection.

MacKenzie's Mills Café

Tammy Tenbult, owner
44 St. Lawrence Street West, Madoc
613–473–1044

Monday through Friday 7 to 4, Saturday 7 to 2, closed Sunday.
Reservations encouraged.

At one time, 125 years ago, Madoc was the town of MacKenzie's Mills, twinned with Madoc in Wales. Today in the very heart of this attractive old town, you will find MacKenzie's Mills, the tea room — a charming room, fresh and clean in burgundy, green and white.

Tammy Tenbult does all the cooking and baking herself, and has a nice, varied menu that changes daily. Daily specials include choices such as cream of asparagus and mushroom soup as well as mulligatawny soup, crab salad on a croissant, chicken or crab Caesar salads with garlic toast, and chicken fingers with oven fries.

Dessert decisions are difficult, as all are tempting — raspberry sour cream pie, banana cream pie, butter tarts, carrot cake, and chocolate–orange cheesecake. The high quality of the food and the warmly welcoming atmosphere make this an excellent place for lunch or dessert and tea.

On the last Friday of each month they are open for theme dinners, featuring a different country's cuisine at each one — Greek, Mediterranean or Italian. Reservations are a must for these special dinners.

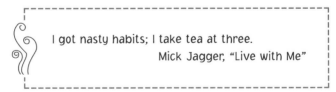

I got nasty habits; I take tea at three.
Mick Jagger, "Live with Me"

The Village Bakeshop and Tea Room

Carol and Gary Vreeker, owners
5340 Main Street, Orono
905-983-9779

Monday through Thursday 8 to 5, Friday 8 to 6, closed Sunday.

Right on the main street of this town, this is a perfect place to stop for tea and a treat just off Highway 35/115 (five minutes north of the 401) en route to Peterborough or Lindsay. Some people put a couple of hours aside on a Saturday afternoon just to drive to Orono for the bakery's goodies.

The tea room is separate from the bustling bakery and is invitingly decorated in country pine, with dusty-pink and white wallpaper, pine bentwood chairs, and Tiffany lamps.

Simple and reasonably priced homemade lunches include soups, kaiser sandwiches, beef pie and sausage rolls. The bakery's treats are all available for dessert — try the lemon coconut macaroon squares that melt in your mouth, or mixed berry crumble squares. Customer favourites are the chelsea buns and the apple fritters. Wedding cakes and special occasion cakes are made to order.

> He traces the steam engine always back to the tea kettle.
> Benjamin Disraeli (1804–1881), Speech before the
> House of Commons, 11 April 1845

> There is a great deal of poetry and fine sentiment in a chest of tea.
> Ralph Waldo Emerson (1803–1882), *Letters and Social Aims*

The Owl and the Pussycat Tea Room

Brenda and David Cutler, owners
127 Walton Street, Port Hope
905–885–8072

Monday 11:30 to 4:30, Thursday through Sunday 11:30 to 4:30, closed
Tuesday and Wednesday.

The Owl and the Pussycat perches on high ground right on the main street of Port Hope, a lovely town of beautiful Victorian houses and interesting shops. Entering this graceful old redbrick house is like stepping back in time to the days when afternoon tea was the highlight of many people's lives.

The tea room has a simple country decor, with café curtains, floral tablecloths and, of course, antiques, a spillover from the thriving antique store the Cutler's run next door.

Here, you can take your time, sit back and indulge in a delicious sandwich, freshly baked scones, or a cake selected from the chalkboard menu. Listed with the daily specials are suggested wines and beers to accompany them. Sweet onion and cheddar quiche, and chicken and seasonal veggies in a light curry sauce in crêpes were two of the appealing specials of the day. Desserts such as carrot cake, apricot coconut crisp with cream, chocolate fudge cake and pineapple date cake with rum butter frosting will satisfy a craving for sweets.

Afternoon tea for two, available all day, is about $8 for four scones, butter and preserves. There is an extra charge for thick cream to complement your scones. You can choose from raisin, sour cream or cheese scones, and some unusual preserves such as pineapple pear or rhubarb ginger.

TEAS SERVED: Orange Pekoe, Earl Grey, English Breakfast, Assam, and Raspberry. Herbal infusions are also available.

The Best of Things

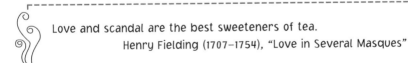

Fran McLaughlin, owner
200 Queen Street, Port Perry
905–985–0170

Monday through Saturday 9:30 to 5, Sunday and holidays 11 to 5.

The day we visited Port Perry, there was a special Satan's Choice meeting, but the heavy security and large number of bikers didn't detract from this wonderfully historic tourist town, which borders on Lake Scugog and has lots of interesting shops. The population is 4,700, but it seems much larger.

Dried flowers hanging from and covering the ceiling draw your eyes immediately up when you walk into this unusual tea room. Antique tables and chairs, a burgundy and forest green decorating scheme, and the selection of gift merchandise — teapots, quilts, topiaries, fresh and dried flowers — all give this tea room an English garden atmosphere. One wants to stay and savour the tea treats and browse for impulse buys. This is a nice tea room and obviously popular with tourists and locals.

The menu offers sandwiches with salad, quiche, meat pies, chicken rotini, and yummy homemade desserts, including date squares, brownies and all kinds of tarts. Seasonal fruit pies are also available as well as carrot cake and cinnamon cake with apple–cider sauce.

LOCAL INTEREST: Visit the Victorian Village or Northwoods Wild Animal Reserve, or tour the downtown area in a horse-drawn wagon.

Love and scandal are the best sweeteners of tea.
Henry Fielding (1707–1754), "Love in Several Masques"

Annabelle's Tea Room

Suzanne Wortman, owner
324 Victoria Road North, Tweed
613–478–3670

Monday through Friday 11:30 to 4, Saturday 9:30 to 5, Sunday 12 to 4.

This large redbrick house, built in 1890 right in the centre of Tweed, is home to Annabelle's Tea Room, a gift shop, a bed and breakfast, and a fabric shop that would thrill any ardent quilter.

Tablecloths depicting country scenes, original wood floors, a beautiful original punched–tin ceiling, and a mix of antique chairs set a traditional theme. The room is light and warm, making it a restful venue for the many tourists, local business people and weary shoppers who tuck into soups with homemade biscuits, sandwiches and delicious home–baked pies, butter tarts and brownies. Lunch for two is about $14.

There are few hours in life more agreeable than the hour dedicated to the ceremony known as afternoon tea.
Henry James (1843–1916), *Portrait of a Lady*

The Calico Tea Room

Freda Shears, owner
36 Jamieson Street, Tweed
613–478–6603

Daily 11 to 4. Only large groups require reservations.

Tweed is a very pretty town with a river at one end and a lake at the other. You'll feel right at home in this cheery tea room. Freda Shears is warmly welcoming and the classical music in the background helps create an oasis of calm. You can relax and treat yourself to a delicious quiche, soup and freshly baked scones, served with jam and cream, or a dessert selected from the handwritten menu. Tea is served in antique china, and the shelves display an attractive collection of teapots and other teawares. There is plenty of space to take tea outside to the huge wraparound porch when the weather is cooperative.

The gift shop adjacent to the tea room offers a delightful selection of linens, handpainted birdhouses and other crafts.

 LOCAL INTEREST: Tweed boasts the smallest jailhouse in North America, just around the corner from the tea room.

We had a kettle; we let it leak:
Our not repairing it made it worse.
We haven't had any tea for a week...
The bottom is out of the Universe.
    Rudyard Kipling, "Natural Theology"

The Primrose Lane Tea Room

The Devonshire Inn on the Lake
Karen and Larry Arbuckle, owners
24 Wharf Street, Wellington
613-399-1851

Saturday and Sunday 11:30 to 4.

This beautiful turn-of-the-century home, built by William Pettet Niles and restored to reflect its original splendour, is situated in the quaint village of Wellington, south of Trenton on the banks of Lake Ontario. Karen and Larry Arbuckle escaped the bustle of Oakville just two years ago to live in this tiny piece of heaven. They opened up their elegant home as a bed and breakfast with five guest rooms (all with baths en suite) and a breakfast room with a deck overlooking the lake.

The tea room, situated at the side of the house and surrounded completely by paned windows, is aptly called Primrose Lane. Karen has stencilled blue-and-white plates and topiaries on the butter-yellow walls. These walls and the sage-green floors, sage tablecloths, and antique china combine to give the room an English ambience that is delightful — and, I must admit, makes this tea room one of my favourites. Glass doors lead outside to a gurgling stream, where a family of ducks has made their home. Throughout the tea room, you'll see refinished antiques for sale; if you're interested, there are more to discover in the small building next door.

English cream tea includes two large scones, Devon cream, home-made jam, and a pot of tea for about $5.

LOCAL INTEREST: Nearby attractions include Sandbanks Provincial Park, golfing, and many antique and pottery shops.

OTHER PLACES TO HAVE TEA IN SOUTHEASTERN ONTARIO

Parkwood Estate, 270 Simcoe Street North, Oshawa, 905–579–1311.
    Luncheon and afternoon tea daily in the Tea House, June
    through September.
Cullen Gardens, 300 Taunton Road West, Whitby, 905–668–6606.
    Lunch and afternoon tea daily.
The Old Country Tea Room and Bakery, 124 Athol Street, Whitby,
    905–668–5775.
Trafalgar Castle, 1 Reynolds Street, Whitby, 905–668–3358.
The Country Shop and Tea Room, Highway 30, Codrington, north of
    Brighton, 613–475–3395.
Cornucopia, 172 Main Street, Picton, 613–476–2702. Afternoon tea,
    Monday through Saturday.

Thunder in the teacup and
Prognostications in the sand
Menaced her amusements with
The abacadabra of death
            George Barker, "Verses for a first birthday"

The Waterford Tea Room

Cathy Toshack, owner
4 Mill Street, Almonte
613-256-3294

Monday through Saturday 9 to 4:30; January and February, Tuesday
through Saturday 9 to 3. Closed two weeks at Christmas.

This is the little tea room that grew. The Waterford Tea Room has been open since 1979, but it keeps growing and growing, most recently adding another room with seating for about twenty-five more people. It has a simple, crisp blue-and-white country decor. All the food is homemade, and that is what the people come back for — Cathy Toshack's home cooking.

Besides the usual soups, salads and sandwiches, the menu is crammed with daily specials, and it would be impossible not to find something you like. Specials that day were chicken divan, broccoli quiche, and salmon asparagus quiche.

The cake selection includes chocolate crunch cake, raspberry ribbon cheesecake cinnamon coffee cake, as well as diabetic bran muffins. Including dessert, two could enjoy lunch in this cheery tea room for about $15.

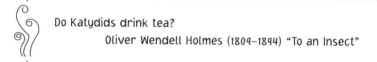

Do Katydids drink tea?
Oliver Wendell Holmes (1809–1894) "To an Insect"

LOCAL INTEREST: Take time to look around at the spectacular waterfalls, the beautiful Mississippi River, the Mississippi Textile Museum, the Lanark Historical Museum, and the birthplace of Dr. James Naismith, the inventor of the game of basketball.

Country Corner Tea Room

Bob and Judy Belton, owners
108 St. Lawrence Street, Merrickville
613-269-4204

Call for hours.

This tea room has a bright country decor in pink and green, and an inviting bricked side patio where you can enjoy your lunch outdoors on fine days.

When we visited, the daily menu offered two quiches — chicken and broccoli or bacon, mushroom, leek and sweet pepper — and two soups — potato leek and gazpacho. Desserts featured were raspberry pie, strawberry–rhubarb pie, and cheesecake. Enjoy fabulous homemade cinnamon buns or scones with your tea.

TEAS SERVED: Orange Pekoe, Irish Breakfast, English Breakfast, Black Currant, Earl Grey, Darjeeling, and Jasmine. Herbal teas offered include Blackberry, Chamomile, Raspberry, Peppermint, and Mandarin Orange.

> It snowed last year too: I made a snowman and my brother knocked it down and I knocked my brother down and then we had tea.
> Dylan Thomas, *A Child's Christmas in Wales*

The Tea Room Café

Steve and Kelly Mulrooney–Cote, owners
224 St. Lawrence Street, Merrickville
613–269–2233

Sunday through Tuesday 8 to 5, Wednesday through Saturday 8 to 9.

Exposed stone walls, sponged forest green and cranberry walls, and very modern local art combine to give this tea room a European bistro atmosphere in which the menu, decor, art, aromas, food and drink are all designed to please the senses. Have a look at the art on display. The owners of this tea room developed Art Aid, a program to promote local artists by exhibiting their work on a rotating basis.

The menu is a little unusual, but deliciously so, featuring sublime salads such as a Thai chicken salad that combines marinated chicken and stir–fried julienned vegetables, topped with a spicy peanut dressing and served on lettuce. Signature sandwiches include unusual combinations such as mesquite smoked chicken served with a light sage–lime spread and tomatoes. Pasta, burgers and appetizers are also on the menu. For teatime there are cheese tea biscuits and scones with butter and jam.

The dessert menu chalkboard is headed up with the words "Resistance is Futile" and "Why not start with dessert and try to save room for salad?" The Tea Room Café is known throughout the area for its tantalizing fresh desserts, made from scratch. Choose from such delectables as bumbleberry pie, blackberry chocolate parfait, berry berry amaretto trifle and chocolate–orange brandied torte with raspberry coulis.

LOCAL INTEREST: Merrickville is known as the "Jewel of the Rideau," as it is such a pretty town situated right on the Rideau Canal. The town is only forty minutes from Ottawa.

The Dream Garden Tea Room

Walter, Ruth and Maya Weibel, owners
106 Main Street West, Merrickville
613–269–2900

Weekdays 10 to 6, 10 to 8 in summer. Closed January.

Situated across the road from the banks of the Rideau Canal, this tea room decorated in soothing shades of pale peach and sage green is home to a Swiss family that has been in Canada for only two years.

The Swiss-style menu at the Dream Garden Tea Room includes open-faced sandwiches served on homemade breads, and quiches, soups and salads. The Weibels prepare baked sandwiches with a twist — unusual yet delicious offerings such as farmer's toast sandwich, a baked sandwich with bacon, pears and Swiss cheese; and asparagus toast sandwich, with Westphalia ham, asparagus and Swiss cheese.

Ice cream desserts are a specialty of the house and include Coupe Jacques, a fruit salad; Coupe Melba, peaches with raspberry sauce; and Coupe Hélène, pears made divine with chocolate sauce. Or you can pick from a daily variety of cakes, pies, muffins, croissants and other fabulous desserts in the showcase.

TEAS SERVED: Earl Grey, English Teatime, Darjeeling, Chamomile, and English Breakfast. Fruit flavoured and herbal teas are also offered.

LOCAL INTEREST: There is much to entertain you in this delightful village: the Block House Museum, Rideau Canal boat cruises, art galleries, a glass-blowing studio and many antique stores.

The Tea Party

Allan Mayer, owner
103 Fourth Avenue, Ottawa
613–238–5031

Monday through Friday 9:30 to 5:30, Saturday 9 to 5:30. Closed Sundays
in the summer; call for open days in January.

Teapots, tea collectibles and tea books fill the shelves of the Tea Party, wonderfully capturing the *Alice in Wonderland* eccentricity of Lewis Carroll's Mad Hatter's tea party.

Allan Mayer has owned this tea room for seven years and has done a splendid job. Everywhere you turn, there is so much to look at — scores of miniature teapots, a fabulous array of novelty, pretty and crazy (as a mad hatter) teapots, tea notecards, tea books, tea cosies, tea tins, tea brooches and tea accessories.

The Tea Party is known for its scones, which the *Ottawa Citizen* dubbed "absolutely the best scones." Everything on the menu is baked on the premises by Allan, and the selection is mouth–watering. The excellent cream tea is about $4 and includes your choice of tea, served in a small Royal Doulton pot, and very rich English scones with whipped cream and raspberry jam or lemon curd.

There is an incredibly wide range of teas and infusions to choose from, and to take home if you wish. You may also find it hard to resist the chocolates, quality preserves, sweets and biscuits that are dis–played on the shelves of the tea room gift shop.

TEAS SERVED: (black) Assam, Ceylon Orange Pekoe, Chinese Keemun, Darjeeling Orange Pekoe, Superior Darjeeling, Dimbula, English Breakfast, Golden Nepal, Irish Breakfast, Kenyan, Lapsang Souchong, Nilgiri, Russian Caravan, Russian Georgian, and Yunnan; and (green) Chun Mee, Formosa Pinhead (Gunpowder), Japanese Cherry, Japanese Panfried, Jasmine with flowers, and Formosa Oolong. Many flavoured and herbal infusions are also available.

LOCAL INTEREST: This neighbourhood, known as the Glebe, is popular for its very upscale, trendy shops.

The Tea Party Fruity Sour Cream Cake

1 1/2 c. all-purpose flour
1/2 c. sugar
1/2 c. butter
1 1/2 tsp. baking powder
1 tsp. vanilla
1 egg, beaten
3 c. berries — try blueberries or strawberries or other fruits. A great idea for Christmas is a raspberry–cranberry mix.

Note: Make sure berries are dry, otherwise the cake will be too runny. Try a combination of fresh and dried berries.

Topping:
2 c. sour cream
1/2 c. sugar
1 tsp. vanilla
1 egg, beaten

Mix all cake ingredients together. Press into a pie plate or 9-inch springform pan. Pour fruit or berries on top. Beat together all topping ingredients. Pour over fruit. Bake at 350°F for one hour. Let set.

Zoe's Tea Room

Château Laurier Hotel, Ottawa
613-241-1414

Weekdays 3 to 5:30, Sunday 4 to 5:30.

The formal menu welcomes you to the ritual known as afternoon tea, "a warm and satisfying Victorian tea, rivaling those found within traditional tea houses of England."

To experience the ultimate in traditional high teas, visit Zoe's in the historic Château Laurier. High tea is served in an atrium elegant with magnificent palms, rattan furniture, and marble. It is named after Zoe Laurier, the wife of Prime Minister Wilfred Laurier. In this 1930s-style tea room, formally clad waiters serve high tea traditionally, on a three-tiered tray. High tea encompasses Victorian scones with Devonshire cream, homemade marmalade, strawberry jam, and dainty triangle sandwiches — English cucumber and cream cheese, smoked turkey with raspberry mayonnaise, and salmon and dill — a slice of afternoon tea cake and a fruit tartlet, and your choice of loose teas. Ports and sherries are also available.

TEAS SERVED: Earl Grey, Orange Pekoe, Irish Breakfast, Lapsang Souchong, Darjeeling, and Jasmine. Herbal and fruit infusions are also available.

Stonebridge Tea Room

Thora and Bob Pugh, owners
Pakenham
613–624–5431

Daily May to October (to Thanksgiving weekend), closed Monday,
starting in September.

What an idyllic setting for a tea room. And set amid the rolling hills along the edge of the Ottawa Valley, with a breathtaking view of the Mississippi River, the Stonebridge Tea Room looks just as it should in a storybook setting. A huge verandah, lush with hanging ferns and spanning the front of the clapboard house, is set with wicker couches and chairs, inviting you to sit for a spell. Inside, soothing pale greens, delightful floral tie–back curtains, parquet floors and fresh flowers make this tea room a tranquil oasis.

The menu offers specials such as cold zucchini apple cauliflower dill soup, spanakopita, seafood red–pepper quiche, and chicken Montebello, and a selection of sandwiches on home–baked country bread. If you can't decide, choose the variety platter — it offers a sampling of sandwiches and a side salad or soup.

Desserts, all home–baked, include raspberry freeze, peach 'n' cream crêpes, orange cake with orange cream, and blueberry-raspberry pie. A cream tea with scones, preserves and Devon cream with tea is available for about $5. Lunch for two with one dessert is approximately $18.

During our ascent of Mount Everest tea constantly gave us cheer and vigour.

Sir Edmund Hilary

Sunday afternoons from 1 to 3, come to Stonebridge's "Music on the Lawn," featuring live bands, rain or shine.

LOCAL INTEREST: Look for Pakenham's unique five-span stone bridge, the only one of its kind in North America. Built by O'Toole and Keating of Ottawa in 1901 with stone taken from a local quarry, it replaced a series of rickety wooden bridges spanning the falls. Walk along the streets following the curve of the river to see the century-old buildings.

Courtyard Tea Room

Audrey and Gordon Durkee, owners
91 Gore Street East, Perth
613-267-5094

Weekdays 10:30 to 4:30, weekends 8 to 4:30. Closed February.

This quaint and comfortable tea room on the main street of Perth is simply decorated, with burgundy wainscotting, original pine floors, brass light fixtures, and dusty-pink tablecloths. At the back of the tea room, a sunny deck with umbrella tables and white wrought-iron furniture overlooks the Tay River.

Audrey Durkee comes in most mornings at 3 A.M. to get all the baking done before the day begins. The breakfast menu lists delicious offerings such as Klondike granola; a breakfast parfait with layers of Klondike granola, creamy yogurt and fresh fruit; orange French toast; cinnamon raisin French toast; Belgian waffles with bacon, sausage or fresh fruit; and breakfast egg crêpes served with a delicious potato carrot pancake, fresh herbs and melted cheddar cheese.

Later in the day, the menu offers homemade soups, salads, and a variety of sandwiches on brown, white, pumpernickel or croissants.

Wonderful home-baked sweets include Mom's Dutch apple pie,

lemon meringue pie (Audrey dares you to find a higher meringue anywhere), chocolate cheesecake, and classic carrot cake. Teatime fare includes a choice of cranberry, black currant or plain scones with jam, or tea biscuits, muffins or toast. Catering and takeout are available.

TEAS SERVED: Orange Pekoe, Earl Grey, Darjeeling, English Breakfast and a selection of herbal teas.

LOCAL INTEREST: Perth is a wonderful tourist town that has not yet given in to the commercialism of many Ontario towns. The picturesque main street, Gore Street, has retained its historical stone buildings. The Tay River, which runs through the centre of town, is part of the Rideau Canal system. The local theatre group and the farmer's market are creatively housed in a glass–and–steel structure overlooking the Tay River that was originally a large bus shelter in Ottawa.

Country Lane Tea Room & Gifts

Sherry Griffiths, owner
243 Castor Street, Russell
613–445–0388

Summer hours: Tuesday through Saturday 10 to 5, Sunday 10 to 4,
closed Monday. From September: Tuesday through Friday 10 to 6,
Saturday and Sunday 10 to 5, closed Monday.

Sherry Griffiths and her husband moved to Russell from Vancouver Island a few years ago to be near their family. The tea room started out in rented space, but once she knew she had the recipe for success, they moved into a house that could be their home and also accommodate the tea room and gift shop.

Sherry likes to appeal to all the senses, providing a bright and cheery decor, perfumed candles, and classical music. The tea room

itself is a cheerful room with original pine floors, dark green trim, green-and-white striped tablecloths, and glass doors across the back leading out to a deck that overlooks a beautiful garden and holds three more tables.

To appeal to our appetites, Sherry offers delicious, but low-fat, low-sodium meals. This tea room takes part in the Heart Smart Program, and so even the cream soups offered on the menu use only two-percent milk. The menu, which changes often, lists such fare as a tea biscuit lunch plate, cinnamon rolls, cream cheese and cucumber sandwiches, and a vegetable salad plate. Homemade baking includes the very decadent carrot cake and frozen raspberry cheesecake. Lunch for two is approximately $15.

The three gift rooms absolutely brim with tempting collectibles toys, candles and framed art. Gift wrapping is done in the swish of a ribbon.

TEAS SERVED: English Breakfast, Earl Grey, Lemon Spice Darjeeling, and herbal teas, including Chamomile and Licorice Spice Herbal.

Royal Albert Tea Room

Colleen and Shelley Sammon, owners
1518 Main Street, Stittsville
613-836-3543

Tuesday through Friday 8 to 4:30, weekends 10 to 4:30, closed Monday.

Stittsville was originally settled in 1824, but after the Great Fire of 1870 destroyed most of the town's buildings, the structure housing this very popular tea room was rebuilt in 1875. The bright, open tea room still has the original punched-tin ceiling. Customers are encouraged to leave their business cards or small advertisements

under the glass tabletops, a clever idea I'd never seen before.

The tea room advises patrons that "each meal is made fresh and takes time to prepare — so relax, and enjoy your visit." All the food is made on the premises by the Sammon sisters — sandwiches, quiches, salads and soups. If you want just a cup of tea and something sweet, pick something from the front pastry counter, perhaps a slice of Snickers pie, Queen Elizabeth cake, berry cobbler, or deep-dish pecan pie.

Afternoon tea is served elegantly, with beautiful Royal Albert china, of course. Cream tea includes tea, tea biscuits, jam and whipped cream; afternoon tea is tea, open-faced sandwiches and a sweet treat.

Teas and Treasures

Eleanor Breese, owner
21 Church Street, Westport
613-273-8327

Monday through Saturday 8 to 4, Sunday 8 to 3.

Westport has only a population of 700, but it is a bustling tourist town, and no wonder. The scenery is absolutely breathtaking. Driving down from Ottawa and Perth, the roads take you down steep, curving hills until suddenly in view is huge, glimmering Newborough Lake and the picturesque village of Westport and its church steeples and old stone buildings. This is truly a hidden gem of Ontario.

Teas and Treasures is a large tea room with a simple country decor — pine tables and chairs and country wallpaper — and a small-town charm.

The breakfast menu, available from 7 to 11 A.M., offers muffins, bagels, eggs, omelettes, home fries, bacon, ham and sausage, as well some rather superb Belgian waffles. Lunch runs to typical tea room

offerings such as French onion soup, salads, quiches, and a hot Reuben sandwich.

Desserts are obviously a specialty, and include apple pie, carrot cake, cheesecake, and strawberry shortcake. Teatime visitors can choose scones and jam, tea biscuits and muffins.

Teas served are: Darjeeling, Earl Grey, Orange Pekoe, English Breakfast and herbal teas.

Moorside Tea Room

Mario Soubliere, manager
MacKenzie King Estate, Valon Street, Chelsea, Quebec
819-827-3405

Daily 11 to 6 year-round. Reservations are encouraged.

This is a guidebook to tea rooms of Southern Ontario, but this historically significant tea room is just across the border, a brief twenty-minute drive from Ottawa, so I am stretching the boundaries a bit to accommodate it in this book.

When William Lyon MacKenzie King came to the Gatineau Hills, he fell in love with the wild landscape, and in 1903, bought a small piece of land on Kingsmere Lake. He eventually owned 231 hectares as well as three summer cottages and a year-round house. In 1928, in his third term as prime minister, King moved to Moorside, a large gracious cottage where he received such guests as Winston Churchill. King added formal flower beds and a hidden rock garden, and assembled from Canada and abroad a collection of picturesque ruins. He also had trails cut through the forest, trails that are still there for visitors to enjoy.

The Moorside Tea Room, open since 1965, has the original tongue-and-groove panelled walls, and large-paned windows and

French doors opening to a patio overlooking the extensive gardens. White tablecloths, white china and fresh flowers, a huge fireplace in the main dining area, and classical chamber music playing in the background make this an elegant, traditional tea room.

Afternoon tea, served daily from 3 to 5, comes with assorted sandwiches, English scones served with whipped cream and preserves, carrot cake bites, a maple sugar tartelette, plus your choice of tea for about $10. Other treats on the menu include tarte maison à la mode — a choice of apple, sugar or lemon cheesecake served with raspberry sauce.

TEAS SERVED: (all loose) Mim-Indian Darjeeling, Earl Grey, English Breakfast, Buckingham Palace Garden Party, Irish Breakfast, Lapsang Souchong, Japanese Fukujyu Green Imperial, and Jasmine tea.

OTHER PLACES TO HAVE TEA IN THE OTTAWA AREA

Bonnie Jane's Scones, 148 John Street North, Arnprior, 613-623-0552.
    Monday through Saturday 8:30 to 5.
Burnstown Café, County Road 2, opposite the post office, Burnstown,
    613-432-8805.
Open May 1 to November 30.
Evergreen Farm, Badell Road, Kemptville, 613-258-5587. Garden tea
    house open summer weekends 10 to 4.
Billings Estate Museum, 2110 Cabot Street, Ottawa, 613-247-4830.
    Traditional afternoon tea on the lawn Sunday through Thursday
    1 to 4, June 1 to Labour Day.
Gallagher House Lakeside Inn, 14 West Water Street, Portland (near
    Westport), 613-272-2895. Luncheon, tea, dinner.
The Old Town Hall Tea Room, 128 Raglan Street South, Renfrew,
    613-432-7971.
Trillium Tea Room, Van Cleek Hill (near Cornwall), 613-678-6892.

JOIN OUR CIRCLE OF FRIEND

The Tetley Tea Circle is a fun-filled newsletter devoted exclusively to the world of tea. In every issue, the Tetley Tea Folk – along with Sarah, the editor – bring you fascinating tea trivia, tips, recipes and a chance to win free tea for a year.

The Tea Circle boasts thousands of members of all ages. And they're found in just about every city and town across Canada. Thanks to the Tea Circle, they stay in touch with Tetley – and each other. They also get advance notice of some of Tetley's most popular collectibles and money-saving Tetley coupons.

If you love Tetley Tea, you should join the Tetley Tea Circle. Here's just a taste of the tea tidbits you'll get in every issue:

TETLEY TEA COLLECTIBLES

In each Tea Circle issue, we offer members the very latest Tetley Tea Collectibles – offered before they're available to anyone else. In the past, we've carried whimsical tea towels, oven mitts, mugs and other items that feature the lovable Tea Folk. New items are introduced all the time so you can add to your collection.

Handy Home Tea Tips

Tetley Tea Circle members are a very handy bunch – they come up with amazing uses for tea. You might want to try these yourself:

- To relieve tired, achy feet, soak them in a tub of diluted, lukewarm Tetley Tea.

- Break open damp Tetley tea bags and sprinkle the contents over any floor that needs to be swept. It really keeps the dust from swirling up.

TEA SUPERSTITIONS

It seems just about everybody has a belief about tea. Here are just two that Tea Circle members have told us about:

•

A bride-to-be will have one son for each teapot she receives as a gift.

•

Never place milk into tea before the sugar or you run the risk of losing a lover.

EA & YOUR HEALTH

Researchers around the world are studying the health benefits of tea and the news is good for tea drinkers erywhere.

Tea contains a unique combination of compounds lower blood pressure and ood cholesterol and stabilize ood sugar.

Studies even suggest that four or more cups of tea a day can wer your risk of stroke.

TEA TRIVIA

Next to water, tea is the most popular beverage in the world. Canadians drink more than *11 billion* cups a year!

There are more than 3,000 varieties of tea, cultivated in 35 countries. Like wines, many take their names from the region where they're grown, like Darjeeling and Assam.

THE CHARMS OF TEA NEWSLETTER

The only Canadian publication about the delights of tea

Tea is no longer a shy, retiring drink. It's for people with a sense of adventure, people who take their tea not just with lemon or sugar or milk, but with flair and whimsy. From weekend shoppers to business executives seeking respite from a busy day, North Americans are finding comfort in rooms with a brew.

The Charms of Tea Newsletter is for tea lovers, tea room owners, tea room travellers, and the tea besotted. Linger over the newsletter with a cup of tea; you'll be transported to an era of gentility with this engaging collection of distinctive articles about tea, updates on tea room openings, tea book reviews, tea etiquette, tea trivia, mail–order tea, and accessories for the tea table. Join tea weekend workshops to network with other tea aficionados.

Join the subscribers across North America who are saying "absolutely fantastic, I read it cover to cover" (Mary Pattison, Publicity, Royal Ontario Museum, Toronto); — "It's great to have a Canadian newsletter to refer to — I thoroughly enjoyed it and look forward to future issues. I just received my first issue — it's great and I already look forward to the next issue" (Kerri Meadows, Courtice, Ontario); and "Well done. I have just received my first copy and love it. It is highly informative, enjoyable, and entertaining to read and feeds my obsession with the ritualistic ceremony of taking tea" (Michelle Coxhead, Toronto).

Send a cheque or money order for $25 to:
The Charms of Tea Newsletter
Box 29029, 55 Wyndham Street North, Guelph, Ontario N1H 8J4
or call 519–836–0620

The Charms of Tea Newsletter is published four times a year.

Index by Location

Index by Tea Room